SWAMP THING

REUNION

ALAN MOORE   RICK VEITCH
STEPHEN BISSETTE   ALFREDO ALCALA
JOHN TOTLEBEN   TOM YEATES

TATJANA WOOD
COLORIST

JOHN COSTANZA
LETTERER

STEPHEN BISSETTE   JOHN TOTLEBEN   BILL SIENKIEWICZ
ORIGINAL COVERS

SWAMP THING CREATED BY LEN WEIN & BERNI WRIGHTSON

swamp thing: reunion. published by dc comics. cover and compilation copyright © 2003 dc comics. all rights reserved. originally published in single magazine form as swamp thing 57-64. copyright © 1987 dc comics. all rights reserved. all characters, their distinctive likenesses and related elements featured in this publication are trademarks of dc comics. the stories, characters and incidents featured in this publication are entirely fictional. dc comics does not read or accept unsolicited submissions of ideas, stories or artwork. dc comics, 1700 broadway, new york, ny 10019. a warner bros. entertainment company. printed in canada. third printing. isbn: 978-1-56389-975-1. cover art by john totleben. publication design by louis prandi.

SUSTAINABLE FORESTRY INITIATIVE   Certified Fiber Sourcing

www.sfiprogram.org

table of contents

SWAMP THING
REUNION

CHAPTER 1

OH NO.

HEY!! HEY, *YOU*! WHAT THE HELL IS *THIS* PLACE DOING HERE? IT WASN'T HERE THREE YEARS AGO!

HUH? SO, WHAT'S THE *PROBLEM*, MATE? A *LOT* OF MALLS LIKE THIS WEREN'T HERE THREE YEARS BACK.

I MEAN, WHERE HAVE YOU *BEEN*, SPORT? IT'S NOT LIKE SOMEWHERE OUT OF THIS *WORLD*.

HEY!

OH GOD, I ONLY HAVE *EIGHT* MINUTES.

DID YOU SEE *THAT?* HE *SHOVED* ME!

WHAT'S THE MATTER, MATE? YOU ON LOCO-WEED OR SOME-THING? WE DON'T NEED NO *YANK* HIPPIES IN HERE, UPSETTING OUR *CUSTOMERS*.

LET'S *SEE*, HOW DOES THIS MATCH UP WITH... AHH, *GOT* IT. *NORTH*, THEN *EAST*...

AND *NO RUNNING IN THE MALL!* I'M TALKING TO *YOU!!*

HMMP.

BLOODY *SPACE CADET*.

OH, I DON'T *BELIEVE* THIS...

OH WELL, OKAY... NOW OVER ON THE *LEFT* IN THE *CORNER*, THAT SHOULD BE...

THE *EXACT* SPOT.

OCCUPIED

AW, HELL.

HEY! HEY, C'MON IN THERE! OPEN *UP!* I HAVE TO GET INTO THIS *CUBICLE!*

HUH?

NOT WITH *ME* YOU AIN'T, MATE, AND I'M STAYIN' PUT!

YOU'LL BE MOVING FURTHER THAN YOU *THINK* UNLESS YOU OPEN THIS *DOOR.*

HUH? IS THAT SOME KIND OF *THREAT*, YOU *DRONGO?* YOU WAIT UNTIL I GET *OUT* OF HERE...

MELBOURNE POST-DISPATCH

REAGAN: "STAR WARS NOT NEGOTIABLE!"

3

I CAN'T...

STREWTH... WHAT THE BLUE...

WHUHH...

I'M SORRY, FRIEND...

...BUT MY NEED IS GREATER THAN THINE.

AAAK!

THAT BLOODY TEARS IT, WHEN A BLOKE CAN'T GET A QUIET PONDER ON THE PORCELAIN.

YOU BLEEDIN' PEROXIDE POOFTAH, I'M GOING TO BOOT YOUR ARSE STRAIGHT INTO BLOODY...

...ORBIT...

HUH?   WHERE...?

...G'DAY?

4

THE MEN'S ROOM FALLS AWAY; ITS WHISPERING ACOUSTICS; ITS CONSPICUOUS LACK OF ODOR, AND THERE IS COLD VACUUM IN MY BONE-MARROW AND HOW BIG AM I AND O GOD, EVERY TIME I FORGET WHAT IT'S LIKE...

...AND FALLING AND FALLING, BUT INWARDS, LIKE SHRINKING, AND THEN...

TENDRILS SQUIRM IN CRUMBLING BROWN PLANET-FLESH...

IN THE LABORATORY, A BOMB, HE BURNED...

THE WHITE-HAIRED WOMAN, GONE...

THE BLUE WORLD, HE JUMPED AND THEN...

WHAT? WHAT? COLLISION! IN NOWHERE. I HIT SOMETHING, IMPACT, THAT SMASHING GREEN FIST, I CAN'T...

⑤

ADAM? ADAM *ILILOC* BA!

MRSMAT! OBSO QU... BAAN *GLISPIN* DOH-HEGER. BAS DRAAT OL HEGER *RANAGAR*.

BAS *OSSI*, SARDATH-CHAT.

TERTEL BU? DUSS MOAL OLT?

O-OL *DHUMER*, CLAAB OL *REKEKI* FAO.

FAOR *APIC-ZETA* FAOR HOORD OL?

BA THOM *ESESSU*. APIC-ZETA THO FAOR *BREMEL* OL HOORD, CLAAB...

FZZZZT

GREEN... SPLASHED THROUGH IT... DEEP GREEN...

SARDATH-CHO! OL *ILILOC*! OL ILILOC *INGLISH!* FAO OL...?

THO. REKEK FAO *WEER*. UNSA *RANAGAR!* MEMEP FAO FAOR *ALDRAAN* OL.

VIER! GLISPIN DOH *RETTE!*

IU, ADAM...

... COLD... WET...

BAS GLISPIN HEGE, SARDATH-CHAT.

AEL! WOAL BAS OL GLAY AMYOR.

... I HIT IT...

FAO THOM HOORD OL...

IU, SARDATH-CHO... FAORI OL AEL-FAO?

SASSU, ALANNA.

SASSU...

CHRUSP

PSSSHH!

D-DUSS MAOL OLT?
FAO ADAM *AEL*?

SA, ADAM
FAO AEL. QU,
DRAL OL *VIER*,
TERTEL BU.

IU, SARDATH-CHO!
BA *ONAMAO* QU!

BA ONAMAO
QU, EMSEC,
ALANNA.

HUHU.

PSSSHH!

ADAM!

IU, ONAMAOL BU...

PSSSHH!

ALANNA.

ADAM, DUSS MAOL? DON-HEGER QU APIC-ZETA WU, CLAAB QU REKEKI FAO.

UH...BA THOM ESESSEN DUSS MAOL. UL TIMTI FAO BA DATTO EPOCHAM APIC-ZETA.

EPOCHAM RIRRIN. EPOCHAM GLUST...

AAN.

BAS UL MASRAUT RAFTI. QU FAO ZON ILILOC HULS CHECHEDOR RANN, DI TOMTA ILILOCTIBANI!

OLF FAO DOH RETTE RANN LEPS THANAGAR.

THANAGAR? THOM KATAR HOL?

THO. THOM KATAR HOL, OOL SHAYERA. OLF FAO HAKKESTRANG! OLF LERM BAAN URDOBAKTI.

RETTE QU ALMASSO.

PSSSHHT!

11

AAN! TERTEL BU DOH RETTE URTH-CHAN!

AEL, SARDATH-CHAT. OL WA ILILOC *THANASARRU,* WO?

⟨ᚱᚾᚷᚷᚷ ᚱᚾᚷᚷ⟩

⟨ᚱᚾᚷᚷᚷ ᚱᚾᚷᚷᚷ⟩⟩⟩

ADAM-CHI! OL FA AELI QU FAO AEL!

OLF FAO KEELA ROO EP SCIRA EK, CHECHEDER LEPS *THANAGAR...*

...ABSORBASCON-LINKED TRANSLATOR SHOULD SIMPLIFY THE DISCUSSIONS.

...ALTHOUGH THERE WAS REALLY NO REASON FOR YOU TO ATTEND THIS MEETING OTHER THAN ALANNA'S *INSIST-ENCE.*

VEEP

YOU SHOULD BE RESTING, AFTER WHAT-EVER HAPPENED IN THE *ZETA BEAM.*

I'M FINE.

GREETINGS, KEELA ROO. MY APOLOGIES, BUT HAVING ONLY RECENTLY ARRIVED, I'M UNFAMILIAR WITH THE SITUATION.

WHAT BRINGS YOU AND SCIRA EK TO *RANN?*

GREETINGS, ADAM STRANGE. WE COME IN RESPONSE TO RANN'S *TRAGEDY.*

TRAGEDY? HAS *KANJAR RO* DONE SOMETHING? OR *HYATHIS?*

NO, ADAM. I FEAR THAT *WE* HAVE DONE SOMETHING TO *OURSELVES...* AN INJURY WORSE THAN ANY INTERSTELLAR *TYRANT* COULD INFLICT.

WATCH THE *VIDELIPSE,* ADAM. THAT SHOULD EXPLAIN.

SINCE OUR NUCLEAR FOLLY MANY CENTURIES AGO, RANN HAS GROWN INCREASINGLY *STERILE.* THERE ARE VAST, BLIGHTED AREAS WHERE NOTHING GROWS; STEADILY EXPANDING *DESERTS...*

IN MANY PLACES, FOOD HAS ENTIRELY *DISAPPEARED.*

RANN IS *STARVING,* ADAM.

12

OH, GOD. HERE TOO? IT'S LIKE *AFRICA*...

I UNDERSTAND AFRICA TO BE A *CONTINENT*. RANN IS AN ENTIRE *PLANET*.

OUR *ABSORBASCON*-GLEANED *KNOWLEDGE* GIVES *THANAGAR* THE TECHNOLOGY TO *RESTORE* THE IRRADIATED *ENVIRONMENT*. HENCE OUR *PRESENCE*.

THANAGAR IS *LENDING* THIS TECHNOLOGY TO RANN?

...AS PART OF A *FREE EXCHANGE* OF INFORMATION, YES.

WE GIVE RANN THE MEANS TO HALT HER *FAMINE*, WHILE IN RETURN RANN SUPPLIES CERTAIN *TECHNICAL INFORMATION* TO *THANAGAR*.

·UH-HUH. WHAT SORT OF TECHNICAL INFORMATION?

OH, MOSTLY JUST *DATA* FOR OUR ARCHIVES. WE THANAGARIANS HOARD FACTS *OBSESSIVELY*...

DETAILS OF RANN'S FASCINATING *ARCHITECTURE*; WONDERS LIKE THE *VANISHING CITY*; THE *ZETA BEAM*; THE *ICE CAVERNS*...

WAIT A MINUTE... THE *ZETA BEAM*? WHY SHOULD *THANAGAR* NEED INFORMATION ABOUT...

MY LORD *SARDATH*, I BEG YOUR *ATTENTION*! RANAGAR IS *THREATENED*!

A *MONSTER*, A *CACTUS* DEMON THAT CAUSES *TERROR* IN OUR *BARTER DISTRICT*...

I SEE.

ADAM, I APOLOGIZE FOR TROUBLING YOU SO SOON AFTER YOUR *DIFFICULT ARRIVAL*, BUT...

YES, YES. IT'S OKAY. I KNOW...

VEEP!

"IT'S A *DIRTY JOB*...

...*CLAAB APOCHAN MASRAUT FAO OL!*"

⑬

⑭

ALPHA IS HUGE AND BLOATED, ALREADY SUNK UP TO ITS WAIST IN THE HORIZON; PROXIMA SMALLER, HIGHER...

I SCORCH ACROSS THE SUNSETS, LEAVING HER ON THE BALCONY WITH HER PERFECT EYES; HER BEHIND, TWINNED EGGS IN MARBLE; HER SCENT...

DAMN. DAMN MONSTERS.

ALWAYS SOMETHING. DUST DEVILS, CACTUS DEMONS...

I HAVEN'T SEEN HER IN MONTHS, ALL THOSE NIGHTS ALONE IN MY TENT UNDER THE STARS, DRIVING MYSELF INSANE THINKING ABOUT HER SHOULDERS, HER NECK...

AND THEN, WHEN WE'RE FINALLY TOGETHER...

WHY CAN'T THESE PEOPLE EVER HANDLE THEIR OWN PROBLEMS? THEY CALL ME NAMES BEHIND MY BACK... APE, THROWBACK... THEN EXPECT ME TO BAIL THEM OUT WHILE...

...WHILE SHE'S BACK THERE, NAKED, TINGLING IN THE SONIC SHOWER...

ARRRGH. MONSTERS!

UGLY, STUPID-LOOKING, BRAINLESS MONSTERS...

I HATE 'EM.

TZU TZU TZU

OOOAAAARRRGH!

⑯

OH FOR GOD'S SAKE.

BETTER LIFT CLEAR BEFORE HE...

SHRAP!

AAAA!

PFUH

HER INTELLIGENCE, HER FUNNINESS, STRENGTH AND FRAILTY...

HER FINGERNAIL, THAT TRACED A BURGUNDY SIGNATURE UPON MY HIP, STILL THERE AFTER ALL THESE MONTHS...

THE MUSCLES SUPPORTING HER RIB CAGE AT THE BACK, WHERE SHE LIKES TO BE TOUCHED...

18

OUT THERE, IN THE CREEPING, ADVANCING DESERT, THE THANAGARIAN SHIP COOLS BENEATH THE SPECKLED BLACK EGGSHELL OF THE NIGHT.

WHAT DO THEY *WANT* HERE? DID THEY SABOTAGE MY ARRIVAL? SO MANY QUESTIONS...

SO MANY MYSTERIES AND...

WHAT? WHO'S *THAT*? CAN'T QUITE...

SARDATH? ARGUING WITH THE HAWK-PEOPLE. SPEAKING THANAGARIAN...CAN'T MAKE OUT WHAT THEY'RE SAYING EXCEPT...

YES. THERE. THEY SAID IT AGAIN. TWO WORDS IN RANAGARIAN: "APIC ZETA."

"ZETA BEAM."

BUT WHY SHOULD THEY WANT THE ZETA BEAM? IT'S ONLY *USEFUL* AS A GATEWAY TO RANN...

GOD, I WISH I COULD TALK TO KATAR. THESE NEW PEOPLE LOOK... I DUNNO. HEAVY. SINISTER. THOSE UNIFORMS...

OH, SARDATH...

SARDATH, WHAT HAVE YOU GOTTEN *INTO*?

NEVER COMFORTABLE WITH THANAGARIANS...TOO HARSH, TOO INTENSE... OH SURE, KATAR AND SHAYERA, BUT OTHERWISE...

KATAR SAID THEY'RE TRAINED TO *KILL*, USING ONLY THOSE WINGS...

MONSTERS. ALWAYS ONE KIND OR ANOTHER: CACTUS MAN; BIRD MAN...

...APE MAN?

SOMETIMES I FORGET. I FORGET THAT I HAVE AN APPENDIX AND SHE DOESN'T; HAIR ON MY BODY WHERE HER PEOPLE HAVE NONE. FORGET THAT HOWEVER WE DRESS, TO THEM...

TO THEM WE'RE ALL MONSTERS.

21

EARTHMAN
ADAM STRANGE
RANN'S
CHAMPION
of CHAMPIONS

NEXT EXILES

LAM *TALSA,* KEELA ROO. QU GLISPI *SARN.*

LAM TALSA, ADAM STRANGE. BAS HAKKESTRANGE *ETHMET* GLISPI SARN.

TOMTEL QU...

BA MURRN ILILOCTA-UNULACON BU...

...SO THAT WE MAY TALK MORE *EASILY.* DO YOU *ALWAYS* RISE SO EARLY TO WATCH SARDATH'S *LIQUID ANIMALS* AT PLAY? I FIND THEM A TRIVIAL AND INANE LIFE FORM.

ONLY WHEN THEY'RE AROUND SARDATH'S IMMEDIATE *FAMILY.* YOU SHOULD SEE THEM WHEN THEY'RE *UPSET.*

KEELA ROO, I NEVER GOT A STRAIGHT *ANSWER* TO MY *QUESTION* YESTER-DAY: WHY ARE YOUR PEOPLE SO INTERESTED IN THE *ZETA BEAM?*

SIMPLE CURIOSITY. YOU KNOW HOW IT IS WITH US *THANAGARIANS...*

I'M NOT SURE I *DO.* I'VE BEEN CLOSE TO *KATAR* AND *SHAYERA HOL* FOR *YEARS,* BUT YOU AND *SCIRA EK* AREN'T *LIKE* THEM.

AH *YES.* THE *HOL* COUPLE. GOOD SOLDIERS ONCE, BUT *IDEOLOGICALLY UNSUITED* TO OUR *NEW THANAGAR.*

THEY PLACE SENTIMENTAL LOYALTY TO AN *ADOPTED PLANET* BEFORE DUTY TO THEIR *HOMEWORLD,* MERGING WITH A FOREIGN *CULTURE.*

IT HAPPENS TO *MANY* EXILES.

"IDEOLOGICALLY UNSUITED"? THINGS HAVE REALLY *CHANGED* FOR YOU HAWKPEOPLE, HAVEN'T THEY?

AS A CULTURE *AGES*, ITS FEATHERS SOMETIMES *DARKEN*.

YOU SOUND SO *SUSPICIOUS* OF US. WE COME MERELY TO HELP *RANN* WITH HER *FAMINE*.

IN RETURN FOR RANN'S *TECHNOLOGY*. YES. VERY *NOBLE* OF YOU.

YOU *SNEER*? WHAT PRICE DO *YOU* EXACT FOR KILLING RANN'S *MONSTERS*?

THEIR *PRINCESS*? A LIFE OF GLAMOR AND PRESTIGE *UNIMAGINABLE* UPON YOUR DREARY PLANET EARTH?

NO, YOU HAVE NO CALL TO MOCK ME. RATHER, WE SHOULD BE *ALLIES*.

IT WOULD BE *UNFORTUNATE* TO FIND OURSELVES IN *CONFLICT* WHEN WE HAVE SO MUCH IN *COMMON*.

WE ARE BOTH *FIGHTERS*, UNLIKE THESE INSIPID *RANNIANS*, WITH MILK FOR BLOOD.

...AND *HERE*, WE ARE *BOTH* EXILES.

GOODBYE, ADAM STRANGE. I SHALL SEE YOU AT *SECONDNOON*, WHEN RANN'S *ELDERS* VOTE UPON OUR *AID* PROPOSAL.

IT IS... MY *PLEASURE*...

I HAD THOUGHT... THAT I MIGHT NEVER HEAR... A HUMAN VOICE AGAIN... LET ALONE...ONE SPEAKING *ENGLISH*...

HOW...DID AN *EARTH-MAN*... EVER FIND HIMSELF... IN SUCH MIRACULOUS *CIRCUMSTANCES*...?

OH, IT HAPPENED *YEARS* AGO. I WAS ACCIDENTALLY ZAPPED BY A *COMMUNICATION BEAM* TRANSMITTED FROM *RANN*... THAT'S *THIS PLACE*...TO *EARTH*.

SOME *FLUKE* EFFECT TELEPORTED ME *HERE*. I'VE BEEN JUMPING BACK AND FORTH EVER *SINCE*.

THIS *"FLUKE"*... HAS BROUGHT GOOD *FORTUNE*... A BEAUTIFUL *WOMAN*... A BEAUTIFUL NEW *WORLD*...

YEAH. I MEAN, WHY SHOULD A *COMMUNICATIONS* BEAM TRANSMIT ME *ANYWHERE*? I WAS *LUCKY*.

STILL *AM*. ALANNA'S LOVELIER THAN *EVER*...ALTHOUGH *RANN'S* SEEN BETTER DAYS...

ALL THIS *DESERT*, IT WAS ONCE *JUNGLE*...BUT CENTURIES AGO, RANN HAD A *TINY, LIMITED* THERMONUCLEAR *WAR*. IT DAMAGED THE ENVIRONMENT *FOREVER*...

VEGETATION WOULDN'T SCARE *RANN* THE WAY IT DID *GOTHAM*. THEY'D *WELCOME* SOME *WILDERNESS!* THEY'D...

UH, LISTEN... ABOUT *KILLING* YOU YESTERDAY...

NO HARD *FEELINGS*, RIGHT?

ADAM? DUSS ILILOC QU AP SMALSH-YEGGER?

ALANNA, BA HET *AMAGLIM!*

EP *URTH,* EPO GOTHAMAGAR, SMALSH-YEGGER FAOR LURSHASTRANG. FAO OL LURSHASTRANG EP *RANN?*

ILI, *ADAM!* OLF FAO *MASGLA!*

YOUR WIFE...SEEMS *EXCITED.* COULD YOU... TRANSLATE...FOR ME...?

I'M *SORRY*...I WAS TELLING HER WHAT HAPPENED IN *GOTHAM.*

LISTEN, RANN IS SUFFERING FROM A *FAMINE.* COULD YOU PROMOTE PLANT GROWTH *HERE,* LIKE YOU DID ON *EARTH?*

MAMOON. ILI, SMALSH-YEGGER, *MAMOON.*

I...DO NOT *KNOW.* I HAVE NEVER...MADE THE *ATTEMPT...* UPON SO LARGE A SCALE... OR SO *DIFFERENT* A WORLD...

BUT... IF YOU WISH...I WILL *TRY...*

THAT'S *GREAT!* ALANNA... SMALSH-YEGGER ILILOC *"TRA"!*

ILI, SMALSH-YEGGER. QU HET *ONAMAS* BA!

LISTEN, WE HAVE TO TELL *SARDATH* THIS. CAN YOU GET TO THE *CONFERENCE CHAMBER* IN HIS *MANSE?* IT'S THAT *BIG* STRUCTURE OVER *THERE...*

IS...THERE *PLANT LIFE* THERE?

NOT *MUCH,* BUT *SOME.* CAN YOU MAKE IT UNDER YOUR OWN *STEAM* OR SHOULD I CALL A *FLIER?*

THERE IS...NO *NEED.* I...SHALL BE THERE... *BEFORE* YOU...

10

IT TAKES ME *LONGER*...TO LOCATE SUITABLE *SUBSTANCE*... THAN I HAD *ANTICIPATED*...AND MY *ARRIVAL*...IN THE *CONFERENCE CHAMBER*...COINCIDES WITH THAT OF *STRANGE*...AND HIS ALIEN *BRIDE*...

THERE IS SO LITTLE... VEGETATION HERE...

I MEET *SARDATH*...CHIEF SCIENTIST...OF *RANAGAR CITY*. HE DISPLAYS...DRY, REPTILIAN *INTEREST*...AS STRANGE TELLS HIM...OF MY WAR WITH *GOTHAM*...

ABOUT US...SIT RANN'S *OTHER* TECHNOCRATS... SIMILAR ENOUGH...TO BE HIS *BROTHERS*... WERE THEY NOT...SO *NUMEROUS*...

I STARE...FASCINATED...AT TWO FABULOUS *BIRD PEOPLE*... ALIEN EMISSARIES OFFERING RANN *FAMINE ASSISTANCE*...

THEY SEEM *FURIOUS*...THAT ANOTHER AID PROPOSAL SHOULD BE CONSIDERED...CONVERSING DARKLY IN A LANGUAGE OF SHARP CLICKS...FEATHERS RUFFLING ...IN AGITATION...

FINALLY, RANAGAR'S ELDERS *VOTE*... SPEAKING WITH ONE VOICE... ALBEIT *MULTIPLE TRACKED*...

THEY CHOOSE ME. SARDATH SHAKES MY HAND... BEFORE A SCREEN UPON WHICH ...PEOPLE DIE FAMILIAR DEATHS... BENEATH UNFAMILIAR *SUNS*...

OFFENDED BY THIS SEEMING *REJECTION*...THE BLACK LEATHER BIRDS...MARCH ABRUPTLY FROM THE CONFERENCE CHAMBER... BLACK WINGTIPS BRUSHING THE CHAMBER FLOOR... EACH STEP A CONTEMPTUOUS *HISS*...

SARDATH TELLS ME...I MAY INSPECT THE DESERT TONIGHT...IF I WISH...

DARKNESS COMES...UNFAMILIAR CONSTELLATIONS FADING INTO VIEW...LIKE DEVELOPING PHOTOGRAPHS...AND STRANGE POINTS OUT *SOL*.

IT LOOKS...LIKE ALL THE *OTHERS*...

HE LEADS ME...TO RANAGAR'S *MARGINS*...TO THE DESERT'S EDGE... WHENCE...I CONTINUE *ALONE*...

11

WITHIN A HUNDRED PACES... I AM ADRIFT... UPON A ROLLING, SENSUOUS LANDSCAPE... WITH DUNES LIKE SLEEPING WOMEN...

THE LISTING HILLOCK OF A SHOULDER... THE HOLLOW OF A BACK... STROKED BY THE WIND'S COLD... LOVING FINGERS...

I TREAD THE SHORES... OF A GLASS LAKE... STILL AND UNRIPPLED... DESPITE THE *BREEZE*...

I IMAGINE... A VAST NUCLEAR FIST... WHITE HOT AND BLINDING... BRUTALLY HAMMERING... THE DULL SAND... INTO THIS FUSED, GLITTERING MIRROR...

I GAZE AT THE *DESERT*... TRYING TO IMAGINE THE *JUNGLE* ... THAT IT *REPLACED*...

FAILING...

A *LIMITED* WAR, HE SAID... A *TINY* WAR...

CHOOSING MY SPOT... I SINK TAPROOTS... THROUGH THE PARCHED TOPSOIL... TO THE *VITALITY* BURIED FAR *BELOW*...

IT IS TIME... I LEARNED THE EXTENT... OF THE DAMAGE...

MY MIND... SLIPS INTO THE *GREEN*...

EXCEPT IT *ISN'T* GREEN...

BROWNS... ORANGES... SOME REDS...

AUTUMN COLORS... THE COLORS OF A WORLD... APPROACHING ITS FINAL *SEASON*...

IS THERE NO *HINT* OF GREEN...? NO *POSSIBILITY*... OF A NEW *SPRING*...?

I CAST THE NET OF MY MIND *WIDER*... SEARCHING *FURTHER*...

PREOCCUPIED... WITH MY INTERNAL *ODYSSEY*... THE OUTER WORLD... SURROUNDING ME... RECEDES... IN MY *ATTENTIONS*...

12

SOMEWHERE FAR, FAR BELOW... WHERE THE RADIATION DID NOT *PENETRATE*... THERE MUST YET BE *LIFE*...

SOME STILL-FERTILE STRATA...THAT REMAIN UNTOUCHED...BY THAT *BLAZING HAND*... OR ITS *POISONOUS SHADOW*...

SOMEWHERE TO THE *SOUTH*...IN RESPONSE TO MY *PROBE*...THERE IS THE BRIEFEST *REVERBERATION*... THE FAINTEST *ECHO* OF *GREEN*... TRYING TO *FOCUS*...ON THE EXACT SPOT... WHERE I EXPERIENCED THE *TREMOR*... I CLOSE IN *RAPIDLY*...

SIFTING THE UNFAMILIAR *IMPULSES*... IS DIFFICULT...AND *CONFUSING*...

I AM *CLOSE*...TO THE LIFE I SEEK...AND YET IT *EVADES* ME. I *HESITATE*...AS IF AWAITING GUIDANCE FROM ABOVE...

ALMOST...ALMOST THERE...

CHOK!

13

I KNEW IT.

KNEW IT AS SOON AS I SAW THAT FLASH OF *VIOLET.*

THEY'VE HIT HIM WITH A *MIND-EATER.*

TYPICAL THANAGARIAN TACTIC. ONE PINS HIM DOWN WHILE THE OTHER DRAWS A COMPUTERIZED *BEAD* ON HIM.

KATAR TOLD ME THANAGARIANS USE *ANCIENT WEAPONS* SO THEIR *ENEMIES* WILL TEND TO *FORGET* HOW MUCH *TECHNOLOGY* THEY POSSESS.

SNEAKY.

IN FACT, A DIRECT *ASSASSINATION ATTEMPT* SEEMS OUT OF *CHARACTER* FOR THEM.

THEY MUST BE *DESPERATE* FOR RANN TO ACCEPT *THEIR* AID PROPOSAL SO THEY CAN HAVE THE *ZETA BEAM.*

I WONDER WHY?

TZU TZU TZU TZU

CRETIN! TELEPORTED ACROSS *SPACE* TO IMPREGNATE THE ROYAL *COW*, BELIEVING IT *ACCIDENTAL*...

STERILE *RANN* NEEDS NO *PROTECTOR*...ONLY THE FIERCE *VITALITY* ENCODED IN YOUR *SEED*...

TALKING, FLAPPING *CLOSER*, SHE SHIFTS HER *WEIGHT* AND I DON'T REALIZE *WHY* UNTIL...

VEEP

WHAT? WHAT'S SHE *TALKING* ABOUT?

=HHUCHH=

NO *GUN?* NO MORE TRICKS WITH YOUR *ROCKET PACK?* YOU ARE EASY *PICKINGS*, ADAM STRANGE. SARDATH IS ABOUT TO LOSE HIS *STUD-APE*.

RIBS. AT LEAST TWO. GOD, SHE'S TAKING ME TO *PIECES*...

WHAT POOR *WARRIORS* YOU TERRANS *ARE*, WITH NO GRASP OF THE EIGHT BASIC *STRATEGIES* OF AERIAL *INERTIA* COMBAT.

WITH *YOU* AND THE ALIEN *DRYAD* GONE, SARDATH'S HYPOCRITICAL *BLEATINGS* WILL *CEASE*.

HE'LL TRADE THE *ZETA BEAM* FOR *ENVIRONMENTAL TECHNOLOGY* OUR *ABSORBASCON* BORROWED FROM *J586*, AND YOUR WORLD SHALL *FALL*.

YOU WILL SOON BE *DEAD*.

SHE'S RIGHT. PAIN *TERRIBLE*... BARELY *CONSCIOUS*, I *DIVE*, THE LIGHTS OF *RANAGAR* CAREENING *TOWARDS* ME...

DON'T *LISTEN*. KEEP *FLYING*. ALMOST *THERE*...

ALMOST THERE.

17

SQUESSSHH

HER WINGS ARE *SODDEN*, HEAVY AND FLIGHTLESS. ONE OF THE ANIMALS POURS ITSELF OUT OF THE *POOL*, COMING *AFTER* HER.

FROM ITS *SIZE*, I THINK IT'S THE *FEMALE*.

SHE SHOULDN'T HAVE *THREATENED* ME. NOT NEAR *THEM*...

IT'S ON HER BEFORE SHE UNDERSTANDS WHAT'S *HAPPENING*. I CAN SEE WHY SARDATH *KEEPS* THEM. THEY'RE MUCH SCARIER THAN *DOGS*.

GLUH

INCREDIBLY, SHE GETS *UP. FLIGHT* REQUIRES BIG *LUNGS*, SO SHE'LL LAST LONGER THAN *MOST*...

SHE STUMBLES ROUND THE GARDEN IN A SLOW FLAILING CIRCLE, THE FLUID ANIMAL KEEPING *PACE* WITH HER.

AFTER THREE MINUTES SHE GOES *LIMP*. AFTER SEVEN IT *RELEASES* HER.

I WHISPER ITS *NAME* AND PET IT, LETTING IT TRICKLE THROUGH MY *FINGERS*. CONTENTED, IT SPLASHES BACK TOWARDS ITS *POOL* AND ITS *MATE*.

POOR KEELA ROO.

WE *TERRANS* MAY NOT BE MUCH ON THE EIGHT BASIC *STRATEGIES* OF AERIAL *INERTIA* TACTICS...

...BUT WE *ARE* COMPLETE BASTARDS.

18

NEXT DAY, THANAGAR SEVERS DIPLOMATIC LINKS WITH RANN AND SARDATH LOOKS DISTINCTLY *RELIEVED.*

THE SWAMP CREATURE HAS RECOVERED FROM THE MIND-EATER. AT *SECOND-DAWN* HE SETS OUT ONCE MORE FOR THE DESERT, SEEKING *FERTILITY.*

BY *FIRSTNOON* HE'S LOCATED A STRATUM OF *UNCONTAMINATED SOIL*, WHICH HE PROMISES TO BRING TO THE *SURFACE.*

FOR MILES AROUND THE CACTUS ROOTS BEGIN TO *WRITHE.* THE GROUND *BOILS* WITH THE PROMISE OF HIDDEN *LIFE...*

FROM CRYOGENIC FREEZERS COME OLD *SEEDS*, SOWN IN NEW *SOIL.*

THE ELEMENTAL FROWNS, CONCENTRATING, AND AS THE FIRST BRIGHT SHOOTS EMERGE, THE OLDER RANAGARIANS WEEP OR APPLAUD.

THE SOWING WAS MIRACULOUS. SHALL THE HARVEST BE LESS SO?

IT'S A *BEGINNING.*

I HOPE RANN CAN *BUILD* FROM THIS AND GRADUALLY RESTORE HER *ECOSTRUCTURE.*

ANYWAY, IT'S BETTER DOING IT LIKE *THIS* THAN TRADING THE *ZETA BEAM* TO *THANAGAR.*

WHY...DID THEY WANT SOMETHING...THAT FUNCTIONS ONLY...AS A GATEWAY TO RANN...OR EARTH...?

EARTH? HMM. I HADN'T *CONSIDERED* THAT ASPECT. YOU DON'T SUPPOSE THEY WERE PLANNING...

NO, NO, THAT'S *RIDICULOUS*...

...ALTHOUGH IF SARDATH *KNEW,* THAT'D EXPLAIN HIS *DISTRESS*...

NO. HE'D *WARN* ME IF THANAGAR WERE PLANNING HOSTILITIES AGAINST EARTH. I'D HAVE *HEARD* SOMETHING...

FORGET IT. FILE IT UNDER *"UNSOLVED MYSTERIES"*... ALONG WITH HOW WE CAN GET *YOU* BACK TO *EARTH.*

RETURNING TO EARTH...IS *USELESS*...WHILE I CANNOT *LIVE* THERE...

I NEED SOMEWHERE... THAT CAN HELP ME CURE ...MY BIO-ELECTRICAL PROBLEMS...

HMM. *KEELA ROO* MENTIONED J586, A PLANET NEAR *MINRAUD* WITH A VEGETABLE CIVILIZATION.

A VEGETABLE... *CIVILIZATION?*

THAT'S RIGHT. HIGHLY *ADVANCED,* TOO, AS I RECALL. MAYBE THEIR TECHNOLOGY COULD HELP YOU.

MINRAUD'S INCONCEIVABLY DISTANT. IT'S WHERE *THESE* CREATURES COME FROM, AND BELIEVE ME, *THEY'RE A LONG* WAY FROM HOME.

AS ARE... WE ALL...

A WHOLE *CIVILIZATION.* I AM *EAGER*... TO *SEE* SUCH A THING.

BUT WHAT OF YOU...? WILL YOU RETURN... TO THE *EARTH*...?

YEAH. ANY TIME NOW. WHY?

20

COULD YOU DELIVER A *MESSAGE* FOR ME...? A *LOUISIANA* WOMAN... NAMED ABIGAIL *CABLE*...

TELL HER... I'M ALIVE... AND THAT ONE DAY... I WILL COME HOME...

PLEASE TELL HER. IT WOULD DO... SO MUCH... TO BRIDGE THE *LIGHT-YEARS*... BETWEEN US...

YES. I CAN IMAGINE. OF COURSE I'LL TELL HER.

MINRAUD'S THAT BRIGHT STAR IN THE NORTHERN SKY.

TAKE CARE OF YOURSELF, FRIEND. THANKS FOR EVERYTHING.

ADAM!

IU, *ADAM!* BA *CHECHEDO* QU!

OH, EDUKU, ALANNA, ONAMAOL BU. BA LAU ILILOC FAOTA AP *SMALSH-YEGGER.* DUSS MAOL...

ADAM, *SASSU.*

BA *MASSIENT!*

21

PREGNANT? BUT...BUT HOW DO YOU KNOW SO *SOON?* IS...

UH, I MEAN, *DUSS FAO QU MASSIENT? DUSS TOMU QU DOH RETTE?*

MASS-LOC BU. IU, ADAM, BA FAO SA GLELIG!

UH, *TRA.* TRA, BAS *APSI.*

IU, ALANNA. SAMSO BA *KLAT...*

IU, ADAM...

BA *ONAMAO* QU.

HER LIPS BENEATH MY TONGUE; HER HIPS BETWEEN MY HANDS; THE GROUND BENEATH MY FEET: ALL MELTING, TO VACUUM, TO NOTHINGNESS...

OH, *NO.*

OH, *PLEASE,* NOT *NOW...*

...BUT THERE'S *ANTARCTICA* INSIDE MY *BONES* AND I'M GETTING *FLASHFORWARD* IMAGES OF SOMEPLACE ON *EARTH,* IN *MOZAMBIQUE...*

...AND I'M *GONE...*

ELSEWHERE IN SARDATH'S *MANSE,* RANAGAR'S IDENTICAL ELDERS TOAST FAMINE'S END... CELEBRATE THE FIRST FRUITFUL RANNIAN WOMB IN...HOW LONG...?

YEARS?

DECADES?

SHE'LL RETURN TO HER CHAMBERS THROUGH SPOTLESS, CHILDLESS PALACE HALLS, MAYBE CONSIDERING WHAT TO TELL OUR OFFSPRING, IF IT SHOULD ASK, ABOUT ITS *FATHER,* SO FAR AWAY...

...WHO VISITS ONLY *SOMETIMES.*

NEXT:

RRRAARRGGGHHH

THE GAME HAS GONE ON, WITHOUT PAUSE, FOR OVER TWO YEARS.

IT IS A GAME WITHOUT FORM OR RULES, DRIVEN BY THE CHAOTIC FRENZY OF ITS PLAYERS TOWARD THE ONLY GOAL THE GAME HAS:

EEEEE!

YYEEEHHAAHHHHH!

PENANCE.

AAAAAEEEEGGH

PENANCE WITHOUT REDEMPTION, AGONY WITHOUT END.

EEEEEEEEEEEEE

UK!

HALFTIME!!!

HIS NAME IS
(NAME? I HAVE A NAME?)
HIS NAME IS GREGORI AR--
(NO! DON'T SPEAK IT, THINK IT!)
HIS NAME IS GREGORI, AND HE SITS READING TO HIS BELOVED DAUGHTER, AND ALL IS RIGHT WITH HIS WORLD.
(BUT MY EYE, IT FEELS SO STRANGE, AND MY KNEES--)

ALL IS RIGHT
(MY EYE, IT FEELS)
WITH HIS WORLD AND HE IS READING TO HIS BELOVED DAUGHTER, ABIGAIL.
(LOOSE, IT FEELS LOOSE, I CAN'T READ WITH IT, IT HURTS)

HE IS READING HER FAVORITE PASSAGE, BEWILDERED AT HOW IMPORTANT IT SEEMS TO HER.
"REMEMBER THAT I AM THY CREATURE; I OUGHT TO BE THY ADAM, BUT I AM RATHER THE FALLEN ANGEL..."

WHY, HE WONDERS, DOES THIS BOOK FASCINATE HER SO? IT DOESN'T SEEM PROPER... THOUGH, AS EVER, HE INDULGES HER.
"...WHOM THOU DRIVEST FROM JOY FOR NO MISDEED. EVERYWHERE I SEE BLISS, FROM WHICH I ALONE AM IRREVOCABLY EXCLUDED."
"I WAS BENEVOLENT AND GOOD; MISERY MADE ME A FIEND. MAKE ME HAPPY, AND I--"
"--I SHALL AGAIN BE VIRTUOUS."

FATHER, WHAT HAPPENED TO THE MONSTER AFTERWARDS? WHERE DID HE GO?
THE BOOK SAYS--

OH, I KNOW WHAT THE BOOK SAYS. IT ISN'T FAIR! I DON'T BELIEVE HE DIED ON THE NORTH POLE. I WANT TO KNOW WHAT *REALLY* HAPPENED TO HIM, FATHER...
...CAN'T YOU THINK OF A *BETTER* ENDING?

③

YOU'VE RUINED THE HAPPY ENDING, FATHER...

SING TO ME, ABIGAIL, SING TO YOUR FATHER...

SHE SINGS TO HIM, AND HIS HEART SOARS WITH HER VOICE...

...AND HE SAVORS THE MOMENT...

...NUUUHH! UH HUN ♪ ♪ HUH NUUUHHH-UH-HUN UH!

JUMPIN' JESUS ON A CRUTCH!

WH-WHAT IS IT?

LOOK, FATHER...

POACHERS! POACHERS ON MY ESTATE!

PLUCHA! NYA UNG PLUCHAS!!

YAAAHHHH!

THEY BOLT AND RUN FROM HIM, HEADING DEEP INTO HIS FOREST...

FATHER! YOU'RE CHASING THEM INTO THE MINE FIELD!!

OH MY LORD...STOP! STOPPPP!!

...HE CALLS TO THEM... THEY HAVE TO LISTEN TO HIM!

FLAH∞ FLAAAAH

FFLLLAAAAA

SPUT

THE MINE FIELD...THEY MUST...STOP...

HE CRIES TO THEM AS LOUDLY AS HE CAN...

...UNTIL HIS LARYNX EXPLODES...

(MY THROAT!)

5

...UNTIL THERE IS NO VOICE TO CRY OUT WITH.

AAAAA

UK

SWAMP THING

created by
LEN WEIN and
BERNIE WRIGHTSON

REUNION

STEPHEN R. BISSETTE   RICK VEITCH & ALFREDO ALCALA   KAREN BERGER   TATJANA WOOD   JOHN COSTANZA
Writer   Artists   Editor   colorist   Letterer
From a plot by: BISSETTE, TOTLEBEN, MOORE and VEITCH

SHE HAD ONCE AGAIN DREAMT OF THE MONSTER. IT HAD COME TO HER IN HER DREAMS, NIGHT AFTER NIGHT, AND SHE HAD RECOGNIZED HIM...

IT WAS...

...IT WAS NOT ALEC.

THE ACHE IN HER THROAT WAS UNBEARABLE.

SHE NURSED THE PAIN IN HER THROAT WITH LIBERAL HELPINGS OF HONEY IN HER TEA.

IF ONLY THE ACHE OF HER LOSS WERE SO EASILY SOOTHED.

6

SHE BRACED HERSELF FOR AN UNPLEASANT DAY. TODAY, OF ALL DAYS, HAD TO START WITH A NIGHTMARE.

NOT THAT SHE HATED HER JOB AT THE NURSING HOME...NO, IT WASN'T THAT.

SHE JUST COULDN'T HELP MISSING THE CHILDREN AT ELYSIUM LAWNS. THOUGH THEY WERE AUTISTIC OR EMOTIONALLY DISTURBED, AND THE WEIGHT OF CARING FOR THEM HAD OFTEN LEFT HER HEARTBROKEN, THEY WERE YOUNG...

...THERE WAS ALWAYS HOPE...

Spanish Acres Home for the Elderly

...WHERE AS HERE...

M-M-MOWNIN', MIZ CABLE.

...HERE IT WAS... DIFFERENT.

GOOD MORNING YOURSELF, AMY. HOW ARE YOU FEE--

STEP ASIDE, LADIES!

OOOOHHH!

OH, AMY, LET ME HELP YOU...

'POLOGIES, LITTLE MISSY!

AWFULLY CLUMSY OF ME--

OOOOHHH, M-M-MY CLOTHES!

M-MY CLOTHES ARE R-RUINED... M-MY GUESTS WILL BE S-SO CROSS--

NOW, AMY, YOU KNOW NOBODY'S COMIN' TO SEE YOU!

--TODAY'S VISITIN' DAY!

AMY, YOU GOT NO FAMILY, NO ONE'S COMIN' TO VISIT YOU TODAY OR ANY DAY.

QUIT YOUR WHINING OR I'LL--

--HAVE TO BE OFF TO SEE TO THE BREAKFAST SERVICE, Y'UNDER- STAND.

YES, GATOR.

ABIGAIL, PROCEED TO MR. JACOBSON'S ROOM AND PREPARE HIM FOR HIS FAMILY'S ARRIVAL. THEY ARE EXPECTED SHORTLY.

S-SURE...UH, MORNING, MISS CLAIBORNE...I'LL SEE TO IT NOW.

HMM...

7

ABIGAIL, COULD YOU ALSO SEE TO AMY'S ATTIRE. YOU REALLY MUST BE MORE CAREFUL, AMY.

♪ AS I WALK THIS LEVEE 'ROUND, I'M LOOKIN' FOR THAT BULLY AN' HE MUST BE FOUND... ♪

HE HAD TO FIND HER

(FIND HER)

BUT IT WAS SO HARD TO CONCENTRATE, SO HARD TO

(SEE, HARD TO SEE, MY EYE FEELS)

KEEP TRACK OF WHAT HE HAD TO DO

(LOOSE, IT HURTS)

THEY HAD DARED TO COME INTO HIS OWN HOME WITH TALK OF TAKING ABIGAIL AWAY FROM HIM... SHE HAD RUN AWAY CRYING... HE COULD HEAR HER STILL...

(M-MY THROAT, TASTING BLOOD)

EVER SINCE ABIGAIL'S MOTHER HAD DIED, HE HAD DONE HIS BEST TO GIVE HER A PROPER HOME. BUT HIS WORK TOOK HIM AWAY OFTEN, AND HIS BROTHER, HIS MEDDLING BROTHER--

--HIS BROTHER AN--

(DON'T DARE SPEAK IT! I HAVE NO BROTHER!!)

-- HAD MADE AN ISSUE OF IT TOO OFTEN... THE AUTHORITIES HAD COME, AND THERE HAD BEEN HARSH WORDS--

(BLOOD IN MY THROAT)

-- AND ABIGAIL RAN CRYING... HE MUST FIND HER...

: SOB :

OH, ABIGAIL...

SHE MUST BE

(FOUND HER!)

FOUND...

8

...MY DAUGHTER...

JA, COME IN!

NOK NOK

ABBY! I'VE JUST FINISHED REPAIRING MISS CLAIBORNE'S WATCH AND I AM ALL READY TO SEE MY FAMILY.

WELL, *ALMOST* READY... I CAN SEE YOU'VE HAD BREAKFAST THIS MORNING...

YOU'RE STILL *WEARING* SOME OF IT, TOWNCLOCK!

ACH, YOU FUSS SO... IFF MY OWN DAUGHTER FUSSED SO, I'D...

I'M SURE SHE'LL FUSS OVER YOU THE *SECOND* SHE'S IN THE DOOR. NOW LET'S CLEAN UP AND HIDE MISS CLAIBORNE'S WATCH. IF *GATOR* SEES IT, IT'LL NEVER GET TO HER!

NEIN, GATOR SHOULD WATCH OUT FOR *ME*, MY DEAR.

AH, ABIGAIL...YOU GREW UP IN THE OLD COUNTRY... LEARNED THE PROPER RESPECT FOR YOUR ELDERS...BUT MY DAUGHTER...MY ILSA...

...SHE DOES NOT CARE. SHE WILL NOT COME.

UH, LOOK, I'M SURE SHE'LL TRY TO BE HERE--

NOK NOK NOK

MR. JACOBSON?

JA? WER IST'S?

YOUR GUESTS.

⑨

...I TRUST YOU ARE PLEASED TO SEE THEM.

JA, JA. COME IN, THERE IS ROOM *FUER ALLES...*

FATHER, IT IS GOOD TO SEE YOU--

UND ILSA? HAS SHE COME?

NEIN...ILSA KOMMT NICHT...

ABIGAIL? WE SHOULD LEAVE MR. JACOBSON AND HIS FAMILY ALONE DURING THEIR VISIT. WOULDN'T YOU AGREE?

UH, SURE... BYE, FOLKS...

SHE THINKS OF THE HURT IN HIS FACE, THE TENSION BETWEEN THEM, AND WISHES SHE HADN'T LEFT HIM ALONE WITH THEM.

SHE THINKS THAT IF HE WERE HER FATHER, SHE WOULD...

SHE CAN'T.

HE'S GONE. HER FATHER HAS BEEN GONE FOR NEARLY FIFTEEN YEARS...

A FLEETING MEMORY, BARELY ABLE TO STIR...

...ERUPTING INTO A GLIMPSE OF THE NIGHTMARE...

...SHE PUSHES IT AWAY IN GUILT AND REVULSION...

10

I—I'M ALL RIGHT... REALLY, I AM...

TAKE IT SLOW, ABIGAIL. DO YOU THINK YOU CAN MAKE IT DOWNSTAIRS?

I...THINK SO...YEAH, I'LL BE FINE... OOOHHH...

I'LL BE DOWN MOMENTARILY TO BREW YOU SOME TEA... CAREFUL, NOW.

FOR A MOMENT SHE THOUGHT SHE WAS IN THE SWAMPS. SHE COULD SMELL THE DANK BLEND OF AIR-BORNE POLLEN AND STAGNANT WATER, HEAR THE HIGH-PITCHED SONG OF THE CICADA...

...AND THEN...

...SHE WAS BACK HERE.

CRICK

HERE, WHERE IT SMELLS OF DUST AND AGE, TINGED WITH THE STINK OF PERSPIRATION AND UNWASHED BEDPANS. HERE, AMIDST THE MURMURING SOUNDS OF LOST MEMORIES AND VACANT ECHOES.

THERE IS NOTHING HERE FOR HER.

SHE ACHES FOR THE SOLACE OF THE SWAMPS...

...ALEC AND THE SWAMPS.

KRAK

GATOR?

UH?

I, UH, FOUND HER LIKE THIS... MUSTA HAD A STROKE... I WAS JUST, UH, CHECKIN' HER PULSE...

LOOK, SHE'S A GONER, BABY... I GOTTA GO CALL AN AMBULANCE...

...YOU FETCH MISSY CLAIBORNE, WOULDJA? LORDY, JUS' 'BOUT EVERY-THING THAT COULD BE WRONG IS WRONG T'DAY!

12

D-DADDY?

HIS NAME IS

(MY FINGERS FEEL BROKEN)

HIS NAME IS GREGORI, AND HE SITS WITH THE MORTAL REMAINS OF HIS BELOVED DAUGHTER, AND EVERYTHING THAT COULD BE WRONG IS WRONG.

(MY EYE, IT HURTS SO, I CAN'T FEEL MY LEGS...)

HE HAD ONCE SPOKEN TO HER, STANDING BEFORE THE FIREPLACE IN THEIR HOME, HER ANGELIC FACE INNOCENTLY ACCEPTING HIS EVERY WORD AS TRUTH.

(I LIED TO HER AND I'VE KILLED HER!)

HE HAD SAID, "MAY YOU NEVER KNOW SORROW, LITTLE ONE--

--AND MAY YOUR HEART ALWAYS BE AS FULL AS IT IS TODAY.

VERBOTEN

D-DADDY? YOU'RE CRYING, DADDY...WHY ARE YOU CRYING, DADDY?

SHE MUSN'T SEE HIM LIKE THIS, MUSN'T SEE HIM IN SUCH PAIN... MUSN'T KNOW THE SORROW OF IT...

D-DADDY? D-DADDY? D-DADDY?

HE MUSN'T LET HER FEEL THE DESPAIR CONSUMING HIM...

(WHY DID I LET HER WANDER INTO THE MINEFIELDS?)

...SHE MUSN'T SEE HIM...

...NOT LIKE THIS...

(GOD, IT'S COME LOOSE, MY--

(--EYE--)

...REACHING OUT...

AMY'S DEAD, I'M AFRAID. A HEART ATTACK... SORRY TO SAY, IT'S AN ALL TOO COMMON EVENT HERE.

OH, GOD... HOW DO YOU STAND IT? I DON'T KNOW IF I--

ABIGAIL, I DON'T MEAN TO BE HARD ON YOU, BUT NEITHER HAVE I TIME TO MOLLYCODDLE YOU. I ASSUMED WHEN YOU ACCEPTED YOUR POSITION HERE YOU *KNEW* HOW DIFFICULT IT MIGHT BE.

IF YOU ARE TO STAY ON, YOU MUST BE ABLE TO STAND IT! I'VE NO USE FOR YOU OTHERWISE.

YOU DON'T SEEM TO LIKE THE PATIENTS, AS IF IT WERE THEIR FAULT THEY ARE OLD AND NEED ATTENTION. IT'S EASY TO GET ALONG WITH THE LIKES OF TOWNCLOCK, BUT THAT ISN'T ENOUGH...

THEY *ALL* NEED CARE AND ACCEPTANCE.

I--IT'S HARD, WITH ALL THAT'S HAPPENED... LIZ LIVING WITH ME, SHE'S PRACTICALLY AN INVALID HERS--

I KNOW WHAT YOU'VE BEEN THROUGH, THOUGH IT'S REALLY NO BUSINESS OF MINE. YOU'VE WORKED WITH AUTISTIC CHILDREN, AND WHEN DEANNA FRENCH GAVE SUCH GOOD REFERENCES, I'D HOPED--

IT'S *DIFFERENT* HERE!

IT'S NOT LIKE WORKING WITH CHILDREN AT *ALL!* THESE PEOPLE--

"*THESE PEOPLE*"-- PEOPLE LIKE YOUR PARENTS, PERHAPS? YOUR FATHER? WOULD YOU BE ABLE TO ACCEPT AND CARE FOR *HIM,* ABIGAIL?

I...

TAKE THE REST OF THE DAY OFF, ABIGAIL, AND THINK ABOUT WHAT YOU WANT TO DO.

YAAAAAAAAAAAAAAAAAAAAAAAAa

KKRRNNG!

WHA-?

15

GSAAAHHHH! LEMMEE GO YOU OL' SONUVA--

WAS WILLST DU DENN HEIR? CAUGHT MIT YOUR HAND IN THE COOKIE JAR, GATOR?

LEMMEE GO!

UNHK.

TOWNCLOCK!

THE OLD COOT HAD IT COMIN'! HIT ME WITH HIS DAMNED KRAUTSTICK!

YOU! YOU WERE AFTER AMY'S RING THIS MORNING... AND NOW WHAT DO YOU WANT, MISS CLAIBORNE'S WATCH?

I CAUGHT HIM, FRAULEIN, STEALING FROM ME...

SHADDUP, YOU BITCH! YOU JUST KEEP IT SHUT!

GOTTA GET SOMETHIN' MORE THAN THE CRAP PAY WE GET TO SHUFFLE THESE STIFFS AROUND! SO'S I TAKE IT! SO SHUT UP!

SUPPOSIN' I TELL EVER'BODY JUST WHO YOU ARE?!! PERVERT!!

MAKIN' IT WITH BIGFOOT IN THE BAYOU! WHORE OF THE BEAST! SWAMP SLUT!

YA HEAR ME--

WE HEAR YOU, GATOR.

I HIRED ABIGAIL KNOWING EXACTLY WHO SHE WAS AND WHAT SHE'D DONE... WHO ARE YOU TO SPEAK ILL OF HER DEEDS?

THE PARAMEDICS ARE WITH POOR AMY NOW. THEY TELL ME HER FINGERS WERE BROKEN AFTER SHE'D SUCCUMBED TO THE STROKE.

WHAT DID YOU TAKE FROM HER, GATOR?

B-BROKE... HER FINGERS?

GOD, NOOOO.

TOWNCLOCK WALKS HER TO HER CAR, SOOTHING HER AS BEST HE CAN. HIS VOICE, HIS TOUCH, THE WORDS OF COMFORT... SHE CANNOT HELP BUT THINK OF HOW HER FATHER USED TO COMFORT HER IN THE SAME MANNER.

HE TELLS HER HIS GRANDSON FINDS HER ATTRACTIVE, AND THAT IF HE WERE A YOUNG MAN HIMSELF...

SOMEHOW, COMING FROM TOWNCLOCK, IT MAKES THINGS WORSE.

16

A PHONE MESSAGE CAME FROM CHESTER WILLIAMS. SHE HADN'T SEEN HIM SINCE THE FUNERAL.

SHE WOULD CALL HIM AS SOON AS SHE GOT HOME, THEN SHE WOULD FIX DINNER FOR LIZ. SHE HADN'T DECIDED WHETHER LIVING WITH LIZ WAS BETTER THAN LIVING ALONE. THE WOMAN REMAINED UTTERLY HELPLESS.

AFTER SHE FED LIZ, SHE WOULD GO OUT.

OUT TO THE SWAMPS.

HE LAY NEXT TO A MOCKERY OF RAGS AND PAPER, AND FOR THE FIRST TIME SAW IT FOR WHAT IT WAS. IF ONLY HE COULD LAUGH.

HE IS THE PATCHWORK MAN, AND HE IS DYING.

HE IS... COMING APART.

SHE NO LONGER CALLED OUT TO HIM, WHICH WAS GOOD. HE DIDN'T WANT HER TO SEE HIM LIKE THIS. HE DIDN'T WANT TO BE A BURDEN TO HER.

SHE CALLED CHESTER AFTER PREPARING SUPPER FOR LIZ.

A SWAMP MONSTER? IN TEXAS!

ABOUT 25 MILES OVER THE BORDER IN THE BAYOUS. TWO KIDS SAW IT THIS MORNING, AND THERE'S BEEN SIGHTINGS IN THE SAME AREA OVER THE PAST MONTH!

I'VE GOT THREE FRIENDS WHO'LL GO WITH US.

BY THE TIME THE RAIN STOPPED HE KNEW WHAT HAD TO BE DONE.

HE WAS VERY TIRED, BUT IT HAD TO BE.

BY 10:30 THEY WERE ON THEIR WAY.

LOOK, ABBY, I DON'T WANT TO GET YOUR HOPES UP.

HE WOULD MAKE HIS OWN BED. DIG HIS OWN GRAVE.

HE WOULD PUT ALL OF HIS FLESH INTO IT.

...AND HE WOULD SLEEP...

HEY, YOU SURE THIS IS IT? MAYBE WE SHOULD GO TALK TO THOSE TWO KIDS AND MAKE SURE. MAYBE EVEN SHOW US THEMSELVES...

ABBY, IT'S 2:30 IN THE MORNING. YOU CAN'T GO WAKING PEOPLE FOR THIS SORT OF THING...

BUT, LOOK, SHOULDN'T WE BE SURE... WHAT IF IT IS ALEC? I MEAN--

COOL YER JETS! LOOK, IT MAY NOT BE ALEC, IT PROBABLY ISN'T. LET'S SPLIT UP AND COVER AS MUCH GROUND AS WE CAN.

MARK YOUR PATHS... MEET BACK HERE IN TWO HOURS, MAX.

MAN, I DON'T FEEL GOOD ABOUT THIS. SHE'S A LITTLE TOO INTENSE.

SHE CAN TAKE CARE OF HERSELF. BUT, I SORTA WISH I'D NEVER CALLED HER... JUST THOUGHT...

IT ISN'T A PROPER BED, REALLY, BUT IT WILL DO.

(SO...TIRED...MY EYE...SO SORE...)

HIS HAND IS LITTLE MORE THAN A SPADE OF FLESH, HIS KNEES WORN RAW, HIS JOINTS SPLINTER WITH EVERY MOTION...

SOON, TO REST, TO SLEEP.

DARE HE LIFT HIS BELOVED LITTLE GIRL IN HIS ARMS?

(A BONE...FROM MY FOREARM...DANGLES BY A STRING OF MUSCLE...)

AND CARRY HER TO BED?

SHE SAYS HER PRAYERS, ASKING GOD TO BLESS EVEN UNCLE ANTON.

(WHERE ARE YOU, ANTON? PUT ME...BACK...)

BEFORE HE LAY HER UNDER THE COVERS

(...TOGETHER...)

AND SHE KISSES HIS CHEEK

(...MY PITTED CHEEK...)

AND ASKS FOR A LULLABY.

WILL YOU SING TO ME, DADDY?

18

I'M GETTING BETTER AT IT... LISTENING TO THE SWAMP.

NOT LIKE YOU OF COURSE, BUT SOMETIMES I CAN HEAR ITS WHISPERINGS, ITS SONGS...

...AND I PRAY IT IS YOU I'M HEARING...

...A FAINT GURGLING, ABOVE THE SEETHING RUSTLE OF REEDS, BETWEEN THE BASS CHORUS OF BULLFROGS AND SOPRANO TWITTERING OF THE PEEPERS. IT ALMOST CARRIES A FAMILIAR MELODY...

I AM COMING.

I FOLLOW THE LISTLESS GURGLING TO ITS SOURCE, HOPING IT WILL SOMEHOW BETRAY YOUR RESURRECTION...

I CAN REMEMBER FINDING YOU EATEN BY RADIATION, CROAKING IN THE DARKNESS... AN INFANT YAM WITH THE VOICE OF A CARTOON CHARACTER... HOW HOPELESS IT SEEMED THEN...

BUT AS I SEE THE WIDE, MOSS-PEPPERED FIGURE KNEELING IN THE DARKNESS, AND WHISPER YOUR NAME--

ALEC?

--I KNOW YOU ARE STILL GONE.

AND YET--

THE HUSHED GURGLING STOPS JUST AS I BEGIN TO MAKE SENSE OF IT. AS IT TURNS, THERE IS A MOIST SNAPPING OF UNWILLING LIMBS AND A FLURRY OF FLIES DISTURBED FROM THEIR FEEDING.

I KNOW IT FROM MY NIGHTMARES.

W-WAIT--

I...KNOW WHAT IT IS...

WHOA!

⑲

THAT'S WHEN IT BEGAN TO RAIN.

STILL, I COULD HEAR IT...

SOB GURGLE SOB SOB

...ABOVE MY OWN SOBBING.

D-DADDY?

D-DADDY?

(I...AM...GREGORI?)

RUN, RUN AWAY, HE'S DYING, OH GOD IT CAN'T BE--

(...MY ABBY...)

(NOOOOOOOOOOO!)

NOOOOOOOO, THIS...CAN'T...BE...

20

THE WET STENCH OF DEATH MELTS INTO MEMORIES OF SCOTCH AND TOBACCO SHE COULD SMELL WHEN HE HELD HER AS A LITTLE GIRL... AND FOR A MOMENT, ALL THAT MATTERS IS THAT HE IS HER FATHER, SHE IS HIS DAUGHTER, AND THEY ARE REUNITED...

COME HOME WITH ME, DADDY, COME HOME--

(I AM GREGORI ARCANE, HOLDING MY DEAREST BLOOD-OF-MY-BLOOD--)

--I'LL MAKE IT BETTER SOMEHOW, I'LL BE BETTER--

(-- I AM STRONG FOR HER, I WILL COMFORT HER, SHELTER HER FROM THE CRUELTIES OF THIS WORLD, I WILL PROTECT YOU, MY LITTLE ABBY--)

--OH IT'S BEEN SO HARD, SO CRUEL, BUT I'VE BEEN STRONG. DADDY, I'VE BEEN THE BEST I CAN BE--

(--FOREVER YOUR FATHER--)

-- CAN'T YOU SEE? I'VE MISSED YOU, NEEDED YOU SO--

(-- FOREVER MY DAUGHTER--LET ME HOLD YOU--)

--THEY KILLED YOU, DADDY, THEY KILLED ALEC, KILLED EVERYONE, EVERYTHING I'VE EVER LOVED--

(-- I LOVE YOU--)

-- MY FATHER--

HE IS GREGORI ARCANE, AND HE BATHES IN HIS LOVE FOR HER, HER LOVE FOR HIM, RUNNING HIS FINGERS OVER HER HAIR...

(--FINGERLESS, ACHING STUMP--)

--DADDY, WHY DIDN'T YOU TELL ME IT WOULD BE SO HARD -- WHY DID YOU GO AND LEAVE ME ALONE?--

(-- I AM WHAT MY BROTHER -- HAS MADE ME--)

-- ALONE WITH SO MUCH SORROW--

(--SHE-- CANNOT-- SEE ME--)

(--LIKE THIS--)

RRRRRIIIP

SHE KNEELS IN THE TORRENTIAL RAINS, REELING, BEFORE CRYING OUT AND FOLLOWING HIM...

SHE SEES HIS LEG GIVE WAY, AND A FLEETING GLIMPSE OF A SPINDLY FIGURE; ITS HEAD IMPOSSIBLY AKIMBO, BEFORE LOSING HIM IN THE DOWNPOUR...

THEN IT BEGAN TO HAIL...

21

CHESTER WILLIAMS AND FRIENDS WAITED AT THE CAR UNTIL DAWN, THEN SET OUT IN SEARCH OF ABBY.

THE RAINS AND POUNDING HAIL MADE FOLLOWING HER TRAIL INCREDIBLY DIFFICULT.

BUT EVENTUALLY, IT BECAME ALL TOO APPARENT...

...ACCOMPANIED BY A DISTANT LULLABY...

...THEY MOVE TOWARD ITS MOURNFUL TUNE OF LOVE LOST...

...A FINAL CHILDLIKE SONG OF ENDLESS SLEEP.

A-ABBY... WHO--

CHESTER... YOU'VE GOT TO *HELP* ME, CHESTER...

...I CAN'T FIND MY FATHER'S HEAD, CHESTER...HIS HEAD IS GONE...

...THE HAIL... HE... FELL APART...AND...

..., I CAN'T FIND HIS HEAD...

SUCH A *WIT* YOU ARE, ANTON, SUCH A REMARKABLE FELLOW TO STILL BE CAUSING *PAIN* ON THE EARTHLY PLANE SO LONG AFTER HAVING LEFT IT YOURSELF.

YOUR POOR NIECE, SHE'LL *NEVER* GET AHEAD...

AH-HAHA

22

GET IT? AHEAD?

HA HA HA HA WHY, YOU'VE *INSPIRED* ME, ANTON! I REALLY SHALL HAVE TO DEVISE SOME *REWARD* FOR YOUR PARTICULAR BRAND OF VILE BEHAVIOR.

WELL, ANTON... THIS ISN'T LIKE *YOU*, NOTHING TO SAY? NOTHING AT *ALL*?

SHALL I TURN YOU OVER TO THE BRAIN WORMS AGAIN? THE IODINE PITS? ANOTHER LAME *PUN*, PERHAPS?

: UH-HUK :

I... HURT HER... : GASP :

ENOUGH! THERE IS NO TRIUMPH IN THIS MOMENT FOR *YOU*, ARCANE! LAUGH IF YOU *CAN!!*

LET AN OCEAN OF DEMONS ENGULF YOU!

LET THE GAMES COMMENCE.

INCREDIBLE...

UNREPENTANT TO THE END, HE'LL BE.

MAY BE PROPER DEMON MATERIAL, MUCH AS I HATE TO ADMIT IT...

ONCE HIS DEBT IS PAID.

"He was soon borne away by the waves and lost in the darkness and distance." —MARY SHELLEY, *FRANKENSTEIN*

NEXT: LOVING THE ALIEN

23

CHAPTER 4

"Quiet, my small. Still your tongue.
Space is all. Space is cold.
You are warm. You are young.
Space is old. Sleep and form.
Sleep and form."

No?

Still awake then?

Does my sleepsong not charm
the thoughts from your minds
and pour them away into the
great-black-outside-that-is-
everything? O, little ones, I am
tired and the blood and ore
move sluggishly within me, but
you: You are awake and restless
in your pods. Slick with warm
oil your cogs and capillaries
prick me as you move.

What disturbs you? Is it the
Dream-Drones that flutter by
your cradles, feeding you their
cool nectar of intelligence, the
chemo-structure of each gleaming
bead encoded with an ocean
of knowledge? Their narrow
beaks drip algebra, cybotany and
a cascade of excellent languages.
Surely they do not keep you
from slumber?

Is it the light? Shall I increase
the number of facets in my
optic canopy and shred its
brilliance still finer?

Is it my voice? Should I remaster
its twelve layers, peeling back
the subsonics?

No.

No, it is not the drones or the
light or my crooning that keep
you from your gentle oblivion.

You are waiting.

You are waiting for me to
tell the story . . .

My story began when the stars were one-tenth of a turn from their current location, and that is a considerable while.

Drowsing in my pod while mother's drones drooled liquid data, I felt my brothers' minds shifting in the chambers beyond my own. Their maleness, their otherness, it excited me, but my mother the island gently chided her only daughter:

"Not yet," she said. "Wait", she said.

"Wait, and you too shall be an island, your brothers as dust-motes by comparison. Wait, and when you are grown I shall launch you all into The Great-Black-Outside-That-Is-Everything. Perhaps one of your kin will find you again; or perhaps those fierce boy-seeds will swim across the blackness to woo some other island's only daughter, just as one of that island's man's sons might come to you, propelling itself through the dark aether with its splendid silver tail.

"Then you will know the ecstasy and the great heat of fusion with one whose flesh is as your own. You will know that melancholy pride which comes with your first pods: Glass bulbs at first; smooth and cold; softened by the fungoid circuitry that swiftly covers them.

"You will know then what it is to be loved, and to be a mother.

"Until then, you must wait.

"Wait."

And I waited.

After some time, I was expelled from my mother's womb of iron and cellulose, spat far into the Great-Black-Outside-That-Is-Everything to await my first lover.

And I waited.

And I waited.

The stars turned by degrees, but no suitors came save those biologically incapable of quenching the longing within me: Alien wayfarers of a myriad different species, perhaps one in a thousand comprehending what it was that he burrowed within. They came, beings made of intelligent ice and creatures fashioned from white sticks and red fibers. They came in loud and smoldering chariots or poured their atoms down beams of blue light.

Some took me for a planet, an unclaimed solar satellite that they might strip the ore from or infest with the overspill of their populations.

Some, perceiving the intricacy of my cyberstructure, concluded that I was perhaps a ship, a giant engine of war that could be tamed and turned upon their enemies.

All of them perished, their chariots and their corpses ground between the gears of a biological process incomprehensible to them, slaughtered by lumbering metal antibodies.

Their flesh was not as mine. I could not fuse with them.

From their remains I abstracted what minerals I could, absorbing them into my own mass. That which I could not ingest decomposes yet within my endless intestinal passageways.

And I wept for them, and for myself.

And I waited.

There in the lonely dark, fear gnawed upon me: Had my race grown fewer across the billennia so that no boy-seeds remained to find me? Had my own brothers perished, searching hopelessly for another island that no longer existed? I ground my continents together in a terrible, bitter frustration. I begged whatever forces there might be that I should not drift for an eternity never knowing love, never knowing fusion, and I waited for their reply.

And I waited.

When my remote sensor globes, afloat in the distant nothingness, relayed to me their first impressions of the life form entering my proximity, I recalled the aliens whose mortal fragments were forever lost within me, and I was not moved.

And yet . . .

. . . and yet there seemed something curious and rare in that swirling pattern of energies, some fascinating singularity. Visually, no physical form could be perceived, no roaring alien craft approaching, and yet my needles danced and trembled in their dials as they recorded each pulse, each fierce surge of its extraordinary vitality.

A blazing star that burned on no visible spectrum, it swam towards me across the Great-Black-Outside-That-Is-Everything.

Upon my hide, a hundred Geysers were silenced and a thousand streams ran dry as I held my breath.

Cheated by this invisible interloper my optic display rippled with mad lights, an agitated brilliance that flashed from screen to screen finding nothing, while all the time I felt that spectral fireball crackling nearer, nearer, white hot and spitting . . .

At the moment of impact a shockwave of foreign sounds and images rang through my being and in that startling, concussive instant I caught the briefest mental glimpse of the invader.

It was symmetrical, its optic canopies two burning wounds in the darkness of their surround. Beneath that, its features were a jumble of indecipherable organs and components for which I had no name. And yet those eyes, those eyes transfixed me, skewered me with their intensity, their great passion . . .

The vision faded almost before it had formed, the intelligence behind it entering the rootclusters and cogs and deep cables of my substance like grounded lightning.

Almost subliminally I noted that there was a fold in the fabric of time at this juncture, and knew that some point in my future would find me performing a chronofracture, but this minor revelation was driven from my mind as my probes grasped blindly for some tangible evidence of the intruder.

There was none.

The intruder possessed no body. He was a ghost.

A ghost that swam through clockwork.

6

Confused, grasping at the quicksilver intelligence with a clumsy fist of neural receptors, I felt again the cold splash of an alien consciousness as its surface thoughts and buried memories washed over me . . .

Buried deeper were darker countenances that had only phobic associations: A half-arachnid form, its one eye filled with depravity; a snarling, feral organism emerging from the skin of another female; a pale and bloodless infant feeding upon its own mother while an aquatic monstrosity looks on hungrily . . .

The faces merged, flowing hypnotically, and when I felt the first twitchings of physical activity within me, I scarcely recognized them.

My cables, unbidden, knotted themselves into tendons.

My cybernetic mosses, wrested from my control, molded themselves into a strange and glittering medium that was not unlike flesh.

The ghost was growing a body, a sentient tumor from the substance of my own.

Nine of my twelve vocal strata rose to the ultrasonic as I began to scream.

And the ghost screamed with me.

From the panic and disorientation that clattered from his mind it was evident that the form he found himself incarnated within was no shape that he had ever anticipated or conceived of.

The slatted vents of my photo-synthetic reactors cast rolling hyphens of colored highlight across the glass exo-skull blossoming from his shoulders . . .

Charting a fluorescent map of the entity's brain I saw creatures like my earlier vision of this insubstantial stranger, and yet NOT like him. They were made of red things, he of green. Foremost was a presence whose upper extremity was shrouded by a mass of white strands. Experiencing a powerful erotic impulse, albeit vicariously, I wondered if this could be the female of the species.

. . . Glinted from the slowly rotating watchworks of a nipple . . .

. . . Sparkled upon the articulated hypodermics of his talons like the rapid, coded speech of signal lanterns . . .

Fully formed now, he twisted and writhed in the striped light, a fabulous and agonized metal sculpture suddenly made animate.

He was beautiful.

He was other.

He was of my flesh.

How shall I say it? How to describe the effect this last bare fact worked in me? He was of my flesh.

I was melted by the implications.

Yes . . . yes, that is it!

"Melted."

Not for my body, that was not melted save for the unchanging magma, boiling ceaselessly around my nuclear core. Not my body, but rather my mind; my psychostructure; my self. My self is what melted.

All the precisely indexed data, sucked greedily from the computer systems of a thousand doomed alien vessels; all my art and science and neurosynthesis; the logarithms and sines; the very formula of what I am . . .

Melted.

It was as if all the electric vapor of my knowledge had condensed, distilled itself back into that trickling nectar that my mother's drones had fed me in the pod.

In my rapture, all my numbers became liquid; I confess I quite forgot the intruder, further to this, I forgot also to stop screaming.

Confused and physically discomforted by my ultrasonics, he ran; lost within a brass honeycomb of service ducts before I could recover myself.

It took only instants for me to triangulate his vitality signals, but by then he had reached the central knot of a transportation matrix used by my maintenance-drones. From the eye of this gigantic and abstract web, spatial wormholes bored their various ways to the ultimate reaches of my body . . .

The icefields of my breast.

The whirlpool-haunted ocean of my brow and the desert of my belly . . .

Peeling back lids of circuit-laced cellulose from the photosensitive steel of new eyes, he watched in terror; in fascination as my drones dug finger-skewers of white gold into the soft plantflesh of their abdomens, cold hands glistening wet, groping amongst their intestines to reset, recalibrate, alter coordinates before entering the pulsing aperture of their choice and vanishing, simply vanishing.

Hoping to recapture him while he stood rooted with incomprehension, I extended eager magnetic digits with rippling fingerprints; tendrils that reached, snatched at him, were too slow . . .

In his retreat from the clutching, shimmering fields of force he stepped into a wormhole and was gone, tumbling without coordinates towards a random destination . . .

I hoped it was not the magma, or, worse yet, the core.

Scanning frantically, blinking eyes like huge frozen ponds, I located his point of exit from the matrix : A service junction on my outermost rind, a false gravity zone. Upon emerging from the wormhole he floundered helplessly, a strange chrome fish thrashing upon an asylum beachhead with no up; no down.

Beneath him, above him, beside him the aerial panorama of a cryptic mechopolis tilted and spun :

The green-tinted roofscape of my hydroponic complex, straining the light of distant suns onto the flowerbeds below, where tin roses with foil petals turned their iridescent, petrol-colored heads, following the light . . .

The pulsating domes and miniature street-illuminations of my drone-cities, where the automata paraded in purposeful silence . . .

A lake of bright mercury in which the dark vanes of adjacent solar windmills hung reflected in still, deep quicksilver . . .

. . . and rearing above, beneath, beside it all, the solemn, ticking colossus of a Time Tower, registering the flux of gravity and regulating the subsequent distortions of regional time.

Across the great pool of mercury a skin-parasite fluttered, lazily, one stained glass wingtip idly slicing the lake's surface yet leaving no scar in the heavy, silver fluid. Scenting the defenseless intruder, adrift in his freefall bedlam, it glided towards him, whisker-filaments twitching thirstily.

He prepared to jump, to abandon his new flesh, his new world, to abandon *me*, to leave me **alone** again . . .

I could not permit that.

It was narrowly timed.

He had already given up his body, reassuming the untouchable mantle of his ghost-form, and if my move were delayed by even an instant, his intelligence would be gone: Parsecs away in a single beat of my atom heart.

I could not, would not lose him now.

I performed a chronofracture.

The time tower supplied all the data necessary to make the incision . . . the stress points in the chronic flux, the places where I could exert gentle pressure, carefully tearing through the skin of time so that I might surgically alter and reset its bones.

As the timewound opened, even the intruder's ethereal form could not escape the howling draft of the tachyon wind, screaming through the aperture and out of that moment, into another . . .

It sucked him shrieking in its wake, out through the rent in the flimsy curtain separating now from then . . .

. . . before from after.

Neatly tying the loose ends of self-fulfilling prophecy into the unfathomable knot of paradox, I deposited the intruder back at the point where I had noted the chronofracture earlier.

Caught by surprise in an event-loop, the staggered and barely conscious intelligence once more sizzled down through my stratosphere while bewildered lights danced across my displays, searching for a visible form when there was none.

Everything went as before: The shock of impact, the almost subliminal first glimpse of his features, the eerie moment when he revealed himself as a phantom, diving bodiless into the cold, oil-scented sea of clockwork, seeking refuge in a fresh-grown body . . .

Everything went as before . . .

. . . except for the part I altered.

Everything went as before . . .

. . . except that this time I was waiting for him.

In the Timetowers the needles convulsed once as I performed the chronofracture breaking the bones of time with exquisite care and subtlety.

My cables, unbidden, knotted themselves into tendons, just as before.

My scintillating mosses became flesh, just as before . . .

After that, everything was different.

His tumor-body wrenched itself free from my cyberloam, snapped wires trailing like ganglia, a rain of microchip soil falling as he uprooted himself, preparing to run . . .

He was too late.

My engines were already surrounding him, presenting faceless walls of frictionless steel, big and indifferent as buildings. A moving city of metal slid towards him, confining him.

Poor thing, that couched his perception of love and lust in such soft and curvilinear imagery, could he comprehend the tenderness in the hard geometric embrace tightening upon him?

I like to think so.

In the blind facade, panels hissed open, leaking steam, and viscous pearls of scented oil trembled on the dilated lips of shutters. From these openings, tongues of thick cable darted, artificial light glinting violet on their lubricated steel jacketing.

One found the intruder's ankle, one a thigh, yet another his shoulder and a fourth his wrist.

As triple-jointed arms of filligree platinum unfolded themselves from niches in the advancing walls and stretched inquiringly towards him, he could not move. His entire being; his strange and singular existence rested wholly upon my whim, was at my disposal. For those moments I owned his life and his death and I loved him for that.

The platinum arm opened its fist and flexed scalpel fingers.

The first cut opened him from throat to abdomen.

He began to gasp and shake, the cables that tied him creaking with the strain. He tried to absent himself from that body, but the shieldfields projected by my monolithic engines kept him caged there, unable to escape, unable to defend himself.

How glorious he was as the pain grasped him by the base of the spine and shook him so that his upper body lashed back and forth in its bonds, the same intoxicating courtship movements that my mother had described in my own father, who, of course, I had never known.

Priceless fingers began to peel away the metal epidermis, pinning the gleaming flaps back with beads of solder, exposing the soft gray plant flesh beneath, small clamps tightening upon the lips of the wound.

The noise that he made was distracting, and might perhaps have spoiled the intimate and romantic ambience of our impending union. Therefore, I modulated my voice and commenced an audial loop of soothing sound-patterns with subsonics that charmed and stupefied the recipient.

After a few moments the screams became low moans and he grew limp upon the torture-harp of wire that held him, hanging in submission, his struggles becoming gradually less frequent as concealed speakers whispered their anaesthetic love songs.

The principal engine moved upon slick bearings into an appropriate position, and as the first stroke of the cylinder heads drove home he threw back his glass-bubble head, and was never more lovely than at that moment.

Finally, with industry and joy and great noise, it was done:

The splendid thing.

The necessary action.

The fusing.

Fine-bore needles of hollow diamond, entering through his gaping scream, struck upwards through the roof of his mouth to fill the cranial cavity with acid. His dissolved brain, in suspension, was then drawn off by the same needles, the stamp of his unique intelligence etched upon each molecule.

At the same time, my cold steel hands worked deep inside his chest, seeking those glands that would become engorged with vital enzymes during this time of unrelenting pain and terror. I liquefied his spine and neural cortex, siphoning the resultant soup away down midnight gulleys and arteries of glass deep within me.

I drank the wine of his intelligence, drank his body; the pattern of his cells. I ate his fear, I ate his agony, I ate his love, his love, his love . . .

The rest I threw away.

Unraveling, the body tumbled down my center-well past level after level, each stratum more cryptic than the one before.

He fell past the tubes of tinted crystal that were already sluicing his codes and his chemicals towards the vats below, where they were analyzed, synthesized and mass produced, channeled along the uterine duct system to be sprayed across my ova-orchards in a fine and fertile mist . . .

He fell past the great industries of my reproductive process, his corpse unwinding into an ungainly tangle of root and wire as his consciousness withdrew . . .

He fell past the depthless secrets of my entire race and their procreation, to him an unreadable manuscript illuminated by fabulous and baffling illustrations . . .

Your transparent pods hung trembling from my iron stems amongst the spiny husks of older and unfertilized eggs, gleaming wet and triumphant and alive amongst those dry, dead failures.

Some of the pods had rapidly acquired their fur of circuitry, twittering drones already floating towards them with cheeks puffed out and mouths full of genius.

In the hothouse of my womb, children were blossoming. *You* were blossoming.

The ghost fell through the whispering, pre-natal twilight, a landscape we recall only in our saddest dreams, and then with a wrench he tore his intelligence free of his dismantled flesh and was gone.

In his time with me, I know not what he saw or how much he understood of it.

If he understood that he was loved, that would be enough . . .

. . . and yet, if he could have lingered, if he could have looked beyond those chip-encrusted pod walls and seen you as I see you now, this cross-section image that coalesces from the phosphordots, ricocheting amongst the latticed rods and cones of my retinal plate . . .

If he could have seen you, the delicate mainsprings of your tiny spines, the infinitesimal cortical clockwork. If he could have seen you, would he see any facet of himself reflected? The darkness of your eyes, perhaps, so like his own? The curve of your shoulders, not yet born and already weary with the world?

Would he have allowed himself to see these things, have confessed to the slightest inherited resemblance?

Could he have loved these lukewarm and peculiar little creatures; these fetal bio-automata; you; his children?

Could your father have loved you?

Yes.

Yes, in time. I am certain of it . . .

. . . but he had to go away.

Away into the great-black-outside-that-is-everything, continuing with his interrupted, imponderable quest towards an unguessable destination.

My surface lenses tracked the burning green star of his disincarnate intelligence as it sparked up through the thin perfume of my atmosphere. My orbiting monitor globes tracked his cometary into the black-ness with eyes that saw far beyond the merely visible, watching unblinkingly until he was gone from all perception . . .

. . . and that is the story, my small ones, of how a barren island called upon the forces that be to end her loneliness, and how the universe responded by delivering to her the succor of a ghost. That is the story of the grand miracle, of the mother whose children were conceived of no tangible father, flesh of no flesh save her own.

You drift and dream, waiting to enter the world, progeny of an invisible god. Your legend will resound down the billennia amongst our kind. Awaiting your glorious coming, I tremble.

Soon, you will be grown, ready to be flung out amongst the unfriendly stars. Already I feel the slow chain reaction escalating by degrees within my nuclear core. When the day is come, the force of my explosion will catapult you deep into the void and your separate destinies, and in that final, white-hot instant I shall be glad, fulfilled beyond all measure.

I knew my fate from the first, my mother's fate before me, that fate sealed by love. It is a universal truth, known to the humblest protozoa: Sex is death. The two are ever intertwined . . .

. . . but you need not think of such things now. The fires of your nativity are still some years away, and for that time of gestation I shall be with you. The fires of your adolescence, though fiercer, are more distant still.

The future will take care of itself. For the present, your mother is old, your mother is tired. Her rivers are barely strong enough to struggle downstream. She must rest now.

Just rest.

Quiet, my small. Still your tongue.

"Space is all, Space is cold
You are warm. You are young.
Space is old. Sleep and form . . .

"Sleep and form."

NEXT: *ALL FLESH IS GRASS*

THE HORROR WAS COMING ACROSS THE STARS.

J.586:

THE LANDLORD TREES OF THE GIANT BANYAM COMPLEX STAND MOTIONLESS, ARMS GROWING INTO EACH OTHER'S SHOULDERS, LISTENING TO THE RESIDENTS LIVING IN THEIR BELLIES.

THE BANYAMS, HEARING ALL THAT OCCURS WITHIN THEM, REPEAT NOTHING.

IN A SUBLIMELY FURNISHED HOLLOW THAT THEY LEASE UPON THE NINTH LEVEL, DISMA AND LOCLISS MATE BEHIND SCREENS OF PAINTED SKIN TO AVOID EMBARRASSING THE ROOM.

IDEALLY MATCHED, PAINFULLY IN LOVE, THEY ARE SURELY THE PERFECT COUPLE.

LOCLISS WORKS IN OLFACTORY DECORATION. DISMA MANAGES A CHEMICAL RESTAURANT. COME FALL, THEY HOPE TO MARRY BEFORE A PRIEST OF O.

FERTILIZATION ACCOMPLISHED, THEY DISENGAGE WITH TENDERNESS, WITH GREAT CARE.

DRESSING, LOCLISS PULLS ON HIS PICKLED GOWN; DISMA HER SHIRT OF ALBINO HAIR. BOTH SAVOR THE INAPPROPRIATE SHYNESS THAT FALLS BETWEEN THEM.

PAINTED SCREENS ARE FOLDED, STACKED AWAY. DIPLOMATICALLY, THE ROOM ASKS IF THEIR SLEEP WAS ENJOYABLE.

THEY NOD, EXCHANGING GLANCES, AND THE BANYAM SMILES INDULGENTLY. THEY STEP THROUGH ITS SMILE INTO THE SULTRY AFTERNOON.

ON THE BRANCHWAY, RUSTLING CROWDS STROLL IN SLANTED SUNLIGHT. TWIGS ENTWINED, THE LOVERS SHUFFLE LAUGHING TO JOIN THEM.

THE HORROR WAS COMING ACROSS THE STARS, INVISIBLE AND WITHOUT A BODY; AN INTANGIBLE KNOT OF MEMORIES, THOUGHTS, IMPULSES...

FOREMOST AMONGST THESE WAS THE HORROR'S URGE TO REACH ITS DESTINATION, THE NAME IT CHASED THROUGH NAMELESS DARKNESS:

J586

THE GALLERY HOLLOW ON LEVEL SEVEN IS CAVERNOUS, ECHO-HAUNTED.

SHURLO THE FLESH-ARTIST GLIDES THROUGH AN ADORING FOREST OF HER ADMIRERS, HALF HEARTEDLY ANSWERING QUESTIONS, ACKNOWLEDG-ING COMPLIMENTS.

A STOUT CONIFER WEARING AN EXPENSIVE FEATHER FACE ASKS HER TO EXPLAIN AN ARRANGEMENT OF DYED MEATS.

SHURLO TELLS HER THAT IT REPRESENTS SOCIAL INTEGRATION, AND THE CONIFER SEEMS SATISFIED.

MERCIFUL O, HOW THEY BORE HER.

SHE WONDERS IF THIS IS THE PRICE EXACTED FOR CRITICAL ACCLAIM; TO BE ALWAYS SURROUNDED BY THIS FATUOUS, WELL-MEANING THICKET, CROWDED UNTIL SHE FEELS ROOTBOUND?

TO BE ALONE. IS THAT TOO MUCH TO ASK?

EXHIBIT TEN: COLORED FISH, INGEN-IOUSLY GRAFTED INTO SYMMETRICAL CLUSTERS. THEY WILL SURVIVE THE EXHIBITION, JUST BARELY.

LOW IN THE SKY BEYOND THE GALLERY WINDOW, MINRAUD IS SILVER AND GORGEOUS.

DECIDING, SHURLO SLIPS OUT BEFORE ANYONE NOTICES.

ALONG THE BRANCHWAY MOVE CREAKING ANCIENTS, PROUD MOTHERS HEAVY WITH FRUIT, YOUNG SAPLINGS DISPLAYING THEIR FASHIONABLE TOPIARY...

HER RELIEF ALLOYED CURIOUSLY WITH AN OBSCURE DISAPPOINTMENT, THE GREAT ARTIST WALKS AMONGST THE COMMON HERD UNRECOGNIZED.

2

THE HORROR DRAWING CLOSER RECALLED TWIN SUNS AND WORDS OF HOPE...

...RECALLED *ANOTHER PLACE*, NEITHER VEGETABLE NOR MINERAL, AND THE HUMILIATIONS SUFFERED THERE...

PUTTING ASIDE WHERE IT HAD *BEEN*, THE HORROR CONCENTRATED SOLELY UPON WHERE IT WAS *GOING*.

"I LOOK UPON THE GAPING NOTHINGNESS AND I SEE O. I COUNT THE RINGS OF MY EXPERIENCE, AND IN EACH I SEE O. I WITNESS THE CIRCULARITY OF ALL THINGS, AND O IS REVEALED IN THEM"

IMREL, SERVANT OF GOD, STANDS ABOVE THE CONGREGATION AND MOVES HIS MOUTH. HE CANNOT BRING HIMSELF TO VOICE THE HYMN:

"I GAZE INTO THE EYE OF MY FELLOW CREATURE, AND O IS THERE..."

IMREL NO LONGER BELIEVES THIS.

THE SPINNEY OF WORSHIPPERS IS DISAPPOINTINGLY SMALL, AND IN THEIR EYES IMREL SEES ONLY CONCEALED PETTINESS, HIDDEN LUST AND GREED.

WHERE? WHERE IS O WHO MADE THE SUNS AND PLANETS IN HIS IMAGE?

NOT THERE. NOT IN THOSE EYES.

THE SERVICE ENDS, THE WORSHIPPERS LEAVE.

FILING PAST HIM, DO THEY NOT SEE HIS DESPAIR? DO THEY NOT COMPREHEND THE FATHOMLESS, FAITHLESS OCEAN IN WHICH HE DROWNS?

MUMBLING ENDLESS PERFUNCTORY FAREWELLS, IMREL DECIDES TO STOP LIVING.

HE WILL HURL HIMSELF FROM THE HEIGHTS OF THE BANYAM COMPLEX, SHATTERING INTO SPLINTERS.

DELIBERATING, HE WATCHES THE PROCESSION ASCEND THE SPIRAL RAMPS...

...THEN, SERVANT OF AN ABSENT GOD, HE FALLS INTO STEP WITH THE SHUFFLING DAMNED.

3

THE HORROR WAS ALMOST THERE.

SINGLE-MINDED, IT KNEW ONLY THE NEARNESS OF ITS DESTINATION, ITS SALVATION.

IT DID NOT KNOW HOW FAR IT HAD TRAVELED. IT DID NOT EVEN KNOW THAT IT WAS A HORROR...

BUT IT WAS.

IN HIS CAVE OF DEAF METAL, FAR FROM THE LISTENING BANYAMS, GREAT MEDPHYL SITS VIGIL OVER HIS MENTOR'S WITHERING REMAINS.

DEAR JOTHRA. HE'D GIVE HIS RING TO WALK BESIDE HIM IN AMIABLE SILENCE, JUST ONCE MORE.

BUT JOTHRA IS GONE.

AND WHAT OF MEDPHYL? WITHOUT HIS TEACHER'S ADVICE, IS MEDPHYL GONE ALSO? THE PEOPLE SAY HE HAS GROWN TOO OLD TO DEFEND THEM: "ONE RING TOO MANY."

RUMORS OF THE GUARDIANS' DECLINE HAVEN'T HELPED...

HE WONDERS IF JS86 EVER NEEDED DEFENDING. ADVANCES IN EUGENICS HAVE ALMOST BRED CRIMINAL TENDENCIES FROM THE POPULATION ALONG WITH DISCOLORED BLOSSOM.

A DAY HAS PASSED SINCE HIS LAST RECHARGING.

HE RECITES HIS OATH WITH LITTLE CONVICTION:

"IN FOREST DARK OR GLADE BEFERNED NO BLADE OF GRASS SHALL GO UNTURNED, LET THOSE THAT HAVE THE DAYLIGHT SPURNED TREAD NOT WHERE THIS GREEN LAMP HAS BURNED."

JOTHRA, JOTHRA IS DEAD.

JUST TO WALK WITH HIM ONCE MORE THROUGH THE NOISELESS LIZARDGARDENS...

IN HIS CAVE OF DEAF METAL, GREAT MEDPHYL WEEPS, AND THE WALLS NEITHER HEAR NOR OFFER CONSOLATION.

4

J586:

ON THE UPPER LEVELS, DISMA BUYS A BOUQUET OF HUMMING-BIRDS AND LOCLISS SMILES AS SHE HANDS HIM THEIR STRINGS.

THE SMILE FREEZES. DISMA IS SCREAMING. GROTESQUELY, HER FLESH BEGINS TO TWIST AND RIPPLE...

THE HORROR IMPACTED WITH THE MOST DENSELY POPULATED SECTION OF THE BANYAM COMPLEX.

UNLIKE WHAT FOLLOWED, THE IMPACT ITSELF WAS SILENT, INVISIBLE, BETRAYED BY NOT THE SLIGHTEST TREMOR.

AS THE SHRIEKING STARTS, SHURLO TURNS TO RUN BUT HER LEGS WILL NOT RESPOND. ONE OF THEM IS STRETCHING, ENTANGLING THE COUPLE BESIDE HER...

EXHIBIT TEN, THE FUSED FISH: THIS IS SHURLO'S LAST COHERENT THOUGHT BEFORE ENTERING PANDEMONIUM.

THE HORROR, REALIZING ITS MISTAKE, ATTEMPTED TO WITHDRAW, BUT IT HAD ALREADY ENGULFED FAR TOO MANY PEOPLE, ITS CONCENTRATION BURIED BENEATH AN AVALANCHE OF VOICES, OF ALIEN PERSONALITIES...

IT WAS TOO LATE. RETREAT WAS IMPOSSIBLE.

THE MOUND OF AMALGAMATED BODIES QUIVERS AS IT STARTS TO RISE, FLAILING LIMBS PROTRUDING FROM ITS SURFACE.

CHEST MERGING WITH THAT OF ANOTHER, IMREL WEEPS AND REALIZES THE INADEQUACY AFFLICTING HIS PREVIOUS VISIONS OF DAMNATION.

TRAPPED IN A NEUROLOGICAL BABEL, THE HORROR UNDER-STOOD THE CATASTROPHE THAT HAD BEFALLEN IT ONLY DIMLY:

THE PLANTLIFE OF J586 DIFFERED FROM THE FLORA IT HAD ANIMATED UPON OTHER WORLDS.

ON J586, THE PLANTLIFE WAS ALREADY SENTIENT.

5

‹ MERCIFUL O, LOOK AT IT! IT IS TOO MUCH FOR THE EYES TO COMPREHEND...›

‹ IT RAMPAGES AS IF MAD. THE BUILDINGS WILL BE DAMAGED...›

‹ THE BANYAMS WILL REGROW, BUT THESE POOR PEOPLE... WHAT OF THEM?›

DISMA? WHERE AM I? ALL THESE VOICES INSIDE MY MIND. IS ONE OF THEM YOURS?

LOCLISS? IS THAT YOU?

...JUST LIKE THE FUSED FISH. THE CROWD. THE CROWD IS INSIDE ME!

...PUNISHED, BECAUSE MY FAITH WAS WEAK...

STOP IT STOP IT STOP IT...

‹ IT'S HEADING TOWARDS THE NURSERY SECTOR. CAN WE SHOOT IT DOWN WITH A BATTERY OF FLAME CANNONS?›

‹ SHOOT IT? MAJOR, THAT HORROR IS MADE OF PEOPLE!›

STOP IT STOP IT STOP IT STOP IT STOP IT

LOCLISS! IT'S YOU! I RECOGNIZE YOUR MEMORIES... THERE'S US, THIS AFTERNOON, BUT FROM YOUR VIEWPOINT.

HELLO? PLEASE, WHO ELSE IS HERE? I'M SHURLO, HAVE YOU HEARD OF ME?

I'VE NEVER BEEN THIS CLOSE TO YOU BEFORE.

STOP IT!

CAST ME INTO THIS HELL, THIS HELL OF OTHER PEOPLE.

NO, NEVER SO CLOSE.

A THOUSAND DIFFERENT VOICES BELLOW IN AN INCOMPREHENSIBLE LANGUAGE, DEAFENING AS ALL THE CHOIRS OF ARMAGEDDON.

HOPELESSLY ENCUMBERED BY THEIR STRINGS, THE FEATHERED BOUQUETS OF THE BIRD VENDORS MAKE FUTILE BIDS FOR FREEDOM...

8

...BUT ESCAPE IS IMPOSSIBLE.

LOCLISS? WHERE ARE WE? I-IT'S LIKE DREAMING EACH OTHER'S *DREAMS*...

US? *RIDICULOUS.* I'M NOT THAT *LIFELESS*...

LOOK, IN THIS *POOL.* THAT'S *US, EMBRACING,* AS WE SEE EACH OTHER. DO...DO I CLING SO *TIGHTLY*?

BUT... THAT'S HOW YOU SEE ME: CLINGING, MANEUVERING YOU INTO *MARRIAGE*...

OH *LOOK!* THEY'RE DWINDLING... GETTING *SMALLER*...

DISMA, I'VE *TRIED* TO BE *RESPONSIVE.* IF YOU'RE NOT *SATISFIED*...

ITS CELLS RAISED DISHARMONIOUS VOICES. THE HORROR *MOANED*...

...AND A THOUSAND VOICES ECHOED ITS LAMENTATION.

FRIGHTENED...

THERE! O'S PRIEST! HE'LL *GUIDE* US...

I...CAN'T. MY FAITH...IT'S *CRIPPLED.*

NO! IT RISES *BEHIND* YOU, *MOUNTAINOUS*...

BIG ENOUGH TO SHELTER *ALL*...

SAFE WITH *FRIENDS.* EVERY-BODY'S THOUGHTS... *WONDERFUL*...

SOME NERVE CLUSTERS INTEGRATED HARMONIOUSLY...

WHILE ELSEWHERE, CACOPHONY ENDURED LONGER.

SUCH *DISTRESS!* WHO?

SHURLO. AN ARTIST...

DID *SHE* HALLUCINATE THAT IMAGE?

NO! THIS PAINTING ISN'T *MINE!* PLANT FORMS ARE TOO *PERSONAL.*

THOSE BLACKENED INSENSITIVE STUMPS, OH, THEY'RE *LONELY*...

SOME PARTICIPANTS SUFFERED NEURAL *PURGATORIES*...

OTHERS FOUND CORTICAL PARADISE.

SEE! WE EMERGE FROM BARREN VALLEYS UNTO GREEN *MEADOWS,* AS O'S BOOK *FORETOLD!*

LOOK! THE STUMPS OF THE *MARTYRS,* SET AT ELYSIUM'S MOUTH!

O! PRAISE *O!*

HEAVEN AND HELL WERE INSIDE IT.

THE HORROR *SCREAMED.*

9

JS86:

ELDERLY CHALQUIS TAKES THE EVENING LIGHT UPON THE UPPER BRANCHWAYS, EXERCISING HIS FAVORITE SHRUB (OF IMMACULATE PEDIGREE BUT QUITE UNINTELLIGENT).

HE ENCOUNTERS OLMUTH, WHEELING HER YEARLING, DULKSMIT. CONDENSATION FOGS THE PLASTIC BUBBLE OF THE CHILD'S GROW-POD.

EVER GARRULOUS, CHALQUIS LISTS HIS SHRUB'S MISDEMEANORS: THE YEARLY SHEDDING; SHAKING POLLEN ON THE POTTED APES IN THE PUBLIC BEASTORCHARDS...

FROM HIS MISTED SACK, DULKSMIT WHIMPERS. PICKING UP THE INFANT, OLMUTH HAPPENS TO GLANCE ALONG THE BOULEVARD...

SOMETHING THAT THREATENS REASON IS RUNNING BETWEEN THE BANYAM BLOCKS.

GATHERING DULKSMIT REFLEXIVELY IN HER BRITTLE ARMS, SHE MAKES FOR THE BRANCHWAY'S FAR SIDE. SHE HEARS CHALQUIS, STUPID WITH TERROR, CALLING HIS SHRUB'S NAME, REPEATEDLY, URGENTLY...

"NOMBICCL!"

"NOMBICCL..."

EVERYTHING IS NOISE THEN, AS THE HORROR PASSES. SHE GLIMPSES HORROR'S SKIN WHICH SEEMS TO MOVE...

JUST TOO LATE TO STOP HERSELF, SHE REALIZES WHY. ALL PRETENSE OF A SAFE UNIVERSE IS PLANED SAVAGELY AWAY, AND OLMUTH SCREAMS.

THE SHRUB COUGHS PLAINTIVELY. THE CHILD SHIVERS AGAINST HER SHOULDER...

SHE AND CHALQUIS STARE NUMBLY ACROSS THE SUDDEN CHASM BETWEEN THEM. IT IS A GULF OF SILENCE, AN EVENT SO LARGE IT CAN NEVER AGAIN BE MENTIONED.

10

ELSEWHERE, AMONGST SHADOWS AND VOICES, LOCLISS AND DISMA OVERLOOK A SIMILAR ABYSS.

PHYSICALLY FUSED WITH HER, LOCLISS SHUDDERS, IMAGINING A LIFETIME OF SUCH PROXIMITY...

...EVEN AS DISMA RECOILS FROM THE YAWNING VOID OF HIS ABSENT PASSIONS.

THE HORROR DREW BACK LIPS MADE OF SMALL BOYS, BARED TEETH THAT WAVED TINY FISTS, FIFTY MAD FACES STARED UNBLINKINGLY FROM BEHIND EACH EYE-LID.

THE VOICES INSIDE IT ARGUED, MOST OF THEM SAID "RUN".

IN THE GALLERY OF SHURLO'S SOUL, ALL THE PICTURES ARE BARREN, ALL THE STATUES ISOLATED.

SHE IS ALONE. SHE HAS ALWAYS BEEN ALONE.

OUTSIDE THE ARTBOUND WALLS OF HER PRISON, THE CROWD SOUNDS SO HAPPY.

THE HORROR SWIPED BLINDLY, GESTURED INARTICULATELY, NOTHING BUT AMOK.

IN EACH HAND A POLITE, WELL-MANNERED FAMILY CLENCHED INTO A FIST OF BITTERNESS AND RECRIMINATION.

THE HORROR RAN, PALMS DAMP WITH ANGRY TEARS, FINGERS QUARRELING.

A CHILD REMEMBERS WEARING WHITE MOTHS IN HER HAIR, A BIRTHDAY TREAT. A VAGRANT WONDERS IF HIS THINNING FOLIAGE WILL LAST THE WINTER.

IMREL TOUCHES EACH ONE, JOINING IN A CIRCLE OF SHARED SENSATION, AND THAT CIRCLE IS O...

THE HORROR TRAMPLED, ON FEET MADE OF CLERKS AND SOLDIERS AND LABORERS...

‹NO! NO, WAIT! WE ARE DELIVERED.›

‹IT'S COMING. WE CAN'T LET IT REACH OUR NURSERIES. PREPARE FLAME CANNONS.›

‹IT IS HE.›

11

...BUT BACK THEN, GREAT MEDPHYL WAS YOUNGER. HIS WILL WAS STRONG, AND THE GREEN FIRE BURNED FIERCE UPON HIS KNUCKLES.

BACK THEN, JOTHRA WAS ALIVE.

〈GREAT MEDPHYL! HE'LL KNOW WHAT TO DO!〉

〈YES... BUT HAS HE THE POWER? IF THE GUARDIANS ARE TRULY DISPERSED...〉

〈MEDPHYL IS OUR CHAMPION...〉

〈MEDPHYL'S OLD.〉

〈YOU'RE RIGHT. "ONE RING TOO MANY"...〉

"ONE RING TOO MANY"...〉

〈GREAT MEDPHYL!〉

OA'S FLAME GUTTERS IN CHANGE'S WIND. IF ONLY THESE FEW LAMPS REMAIN TO LIGHT A DARKENING COSMOS, CAN THERE EVER BE ONE RING TOO MANY?

NO. NO, OF COURSE NOT.

〈NO, MEDPHYL WILL SAVE US. IN THE GREAT QUAKE OF '05 HE WRESTLED A CONTINENT...〉

COMMITTED, GREEN LANTERN RAISES HIS HAND.

12

AND THE HORROR IS CORED BY AN EXPERT BLADE OF EMERALD AND...

...AND DOZENS ARE SLICED FROM BUD TO ROOT, AND THE GUTTERS ARE STICKY WITH THE SAP OF INNOCENTS...

NO.

NOT VIOLENCE. RESTRAINT?

AND GREAT MEDPHYL CLENCHES HIS MIND AND THE HORROR IS MANACLED BY SHACKLES OF GREEN UNDERWATER LIGHT, AND...

...AND CHILDREN ARE CRUSHED AGAINST AN UNYIELDING PHOSPHORESCENT, SPLINTERING AS THE MONSTER STRUGGLES AGAINST HIS CHAINS...

NO. SOMETHING ELSE. STUNNING IT, PERHAPS...

...AND THE HORROR STAGGERS, THEN TOPPLES, AN AVALANCHE OF SCREAMING TIMBER, A LOGSLIDE OF PEOPLE, AND THEIR UNIDENTIFIABLE FRAGMENTS ARE SCATTERED OVER SEVERAL BLOCKS...

NO, NO, NO, NO!

NOTHING'S HAPPENING!

GREAT MEDPHYL! HELP US!

LOOK AT HIM! FROZEN LIKE A PETRIFIED FERN!

WHY DOESN'T HE DO SOMETHING?

13

IF ONLY *JOTHRA* WERE HERE, WITH HIS MARTIAL SKILLS, HIS WISDOM...

"*CONFLICT* ITSELF IS YOUR ONLY TRUE FOE. YOU CANNOT DEFEAT IT BY *PHYSICAL FORCE,* BECAUSE IT *IS* PHYSICAL FORCE. TO DEFEAT CONFLICT, YOU MUST ENGAGE YOUR OPPONENT'S *MIND...*"

ENGAGE THE *MIND...*

TOUCHING THE *FLESH* ENDANGERS INNOCENTS, YET BURIED BENEATH THAT MOUNTAIN OF INNOCENTS MUST BE THE *MIND...* THE AMALGAMATING FORCE THAT *ANIMATES* THEM SO GROTESQUELY...

THE GREEN LANTERN OF *JS86* CONCENTRATES...

...AND HIS *WILL* IS A TERRIBLE, ROARING THING, A COLD SUNBURST PERCHED UPON HIS *FIST...*

A *HANDFUL* OF EXTRAORDINARY LIGHTS.

MORE DAZZLING THAN THE FRIGHTENING CROWNS OF *ELMO'S FIRE* THE SKY SOMETIMES BESTOWED UPON TALLER *BANYAMS,* MORE FASCINATING THAN A LIGHTNING-EMBROIDERED NIGHT, THE BRILLIANCE DANCES.

THE *ONLOOKERS* ARE A MOTIONLESS *FOREST,* SUCH AS MIGHT NOT BE FOUND THROUGHOUT THE BREADTH OF *JS86.*

14

THE HORROR PAUSES, CAPTIVATED BY A MOIRÉ OF FLUORESCENT LIME. TO EITHER SIDE PULSE STROBES OF ELECTRIC JADE. CAREFULLY, MEDPHYL INCREASES THEIR FREQUENCY.

AT NINETEEN CYCLES PER SECOND THE HORROR BECOMES RIGID, TRANSFIXED...

THE MIND OF ANY CORPORATE ENTITY MUST HARBOR SOME DEGREE OF CONFUSION. A CONFUSED MIND IS NOT DIFFICULT TO DISTRACT, OFFERING LITTLE RESISTANCE.

THUS DISTRACTED, THE HORROR MAY PERHAPS BE DISMANTLED.

THIS, AT LEAST, IS MEDPHYL'S PLAN.

THROUGH THE SHIMMERING GLAMOUR, THE GREEN LANTERN EXTRUDES RAY TENTACLES, POWERFUL AND SENSITIVE, ALL THE WHILE MAINTAINING THE STROBING OPTIC DISPLAY.

WITH SOME SATISFACTION HE NOTES THAT HE'D NOT HAVE DARED ATTEMPT THIS AS A YOUNGER BEING.

LIKE A SHARK-FARMER ABOUT HIS HARVEST, MEDPHYL HAULS UPON A DOZEN LINES, REELING IN EACH RECLAIMED SOUL AS GREEN PHOTON FINGERS UNTANGLE IT FROM THE MESMERIZED CENTRAL MASS.

THE DISMANTLING BEGINS.

UNTANGLED, SET GENTLY DOWN ON GREEN THREADS FROM ABOVE, DISMA AND LOCLISS SEEK WORDS WHERE NO WORDS REMAIN.

THEY KNOW EACH OTHER, INTIMATELY; CRUSHINGLY. NOTHING REMAINS TO BE SAID.

SHE IS THE FIRST TO TURN AWAY, JUST.

UNRAVELED TO THE CHEST, THE HORROR'S HEART FLIES INTO PIECES, EACH FRAGMENT LOWERED TO SOLID EARTH AS THOUGH IT WERE PORCELAIN.

MELTING IN A LUMINOUS RAIN, THE HORROR'S BREAST IS TORN, SPILLING PEOPLE.

CHILDREN GATHER ABOUT IMREL'S LEGS, CLUTCHING AT HIS ROBE, AND HIS SPIRIT SOARS.

THEIR FACES ARE TURNED UP TO WATCH THE PYROTECHNIC MARVEL OF THE HEAVENS, EACH MOUTH FROZEN INTO THE SAME DIVINE SYLLABLE:

'O.'

NOW ONLY ITS FEET REMAIN, WHERE THE GREATEST INJURIES HAVE BEEN SUSTAINED, THOUGH WITHOUT FATALITY.

BINDING FRACTURES AS BEST HE CAN, MEDPHYL REFLECTS UPON THAT PART OF THE HORROR LEFT WHEN THE PEOPLE HAVE BEEN PARED AWAY.

AMONGST THE LAST RESCUED, SHURLO FINDS THE CROWD ALREADY DISPERSING, DISCUSSING THEIR SHARED EXPERIENCE AS THEY WANDER AWAY TOGETHER.

SCARCELY HESITATING, SHE RUNS TO FOLLOW.

IF THEY REJECT HER, THERE'S ALWAYS THE HIGHEST LEVELS, THE LONGEST DROP...

ITS COMPONENT ATOMS SCATTER, RETURNING TO THEIR FAMILIES AND LIVES. ONLY ITS ESSENCE LINGERS, A WEB OF KNOTTED LIGHT STRUNG ON EMPTY AIR.

SEALED INSIDE A GREEN GLASS JAR, GREAT MEDPHYL SAVES THE HORROR'S SOUL FOR LATER.

16

LATER:

GREETINGS. IF YOU ARE CAPABLE OF VERBAL COMMUNICATION, MY RING SHOULD BE TRANSLATING FOR YOU.

I AM *MEDPHYL,* THE *GREEN LANTERN* OF *J586.*

THE QUESTION *IS,* I THINK, WHAT IN O'S NAME ARE *YOU?*

I AM... THE *SWAMP THING*... OF PLANET *EARTH*... A CHANGE... IN MY *BIO-ELECTRICAL PATTERN*... HAS MADE ME *INCOMPATIBLE*... WITH MY OWN WORLD...

I AM CONDEMNED... TO WANDER THE *STARS*... SEEKING A *CURE*...

AND CAUSING *HAVOC?*

I AM... TRULY SORRY. I DID NOT REALIZE... THAT ALL PLANTS HERE... ARE SENTIENT...

HAVING FORMED A *BODY*... MY MIND WAS *SUBMERGED*... IN A *MASS PANIC*... TOO *CONFUSED*... TO *WITHDRAW*...

PLEASE... I WAS TOLD... I MIGHT FIND HELP ON *J586.*

WE HAVE *DISCIPLINES* TO MODIFY THE *VIBRATIONAL* RATE OF THE *BIO-FIELD,* IF THAT WOULD *RID* US OF YOU.

LEARNING THEM WOULD TAKE TIME!

I AM *RELUCTANT*... TO REMAIN INCARNATE FOR TOO LONG... WITH NO *VEGETATION*... I CAN SAFELY *INHABIT*...

...WITH NO PROSPECT... OF A *BODY*...

17

...AND IN HIS CAVE OF MUTE IRON AND DISCRETE ROCK, GREAT MEDPHYL'S SAP CHURNS WITH AN INDECISION UNKNOWN SINCE FIRST HE FATHOMED THE WEIRD OF THE GREEN LAMP...

...AND FINALLY HE DECIDES THAT YES, IT'S BLASPHEMY, OF COURSE IT'S BLASPHEMY...

...AND SUGGESTS IT ANYWAY...

...AND OH, SEE, THERE, HIS HAND, JOTHRA'S HAND IS MOVING...

TO WALK WITH HIM ONCE MORE IN THE KNOWING SILENCE BETWEEN THE THORNY CLUSTERS OF ROTTING SUNGAZERS, PAST WHERE THE GILAS SPRAWL LIKE OVERRIPE FRUIT, YELLOW AND BLACK AND POISONOUS...

THEIR AMMONIAC AROMA IS HEAVY AND SENSUAL, PERMEATING THE LONG AFTERNOONS WITH AN EX-QUISITE, UNBEARABLE NOSTALGIA.

BY NIGHT, IN THE CAVERN OF LAMPS, GREAT MEDPHYL WATCHES THE LIVING LIGHTNING OSCILLATE UPON ITS SENSOR-PEDESTAL, AS ANTIQUE DEMONS DANCE IN THEIR CHALK CIRCLES...

OBSERVING A FEEDBACK SCREEN-IMAGE OF ITS WAVE PATTERNS IT NOTES THEIR CHANGES AND LEARNS TO CONTROL THEM.

UNFETTERED BY BASE SUBSTANCE IT LEARS, BURNS, IS GLORIOUS; THE VERY SOUL OF THE GREAT LANTERN ITSELF...

18

THROUGH GLADES OF JEWELLED LACERTAS, COOL AND OCEAN-GREEN, PRETTY FEMALES GLIDE IN CONVER-SATION, WEARING SPRAYS TO MASK THE SCENT OF THEIR FLOWERS FOR MODESTY'S SAKE. JOTHRA SEEMS TO SMILE, REMINISCENTLY.

MEDPHYL BASKS IN HIS MENTOR'S PRESENCE, RECALLING HIS HUMOR, HIS KINDLINESS. JOTHRA WOULD EAT ONLY ANIMALS, NEVER THE FLESH OF THE LOWER VEGETABLES.

THE MEMORIES ARE GLAD AND PLENTIFUL, AND SO THE DAYS PASS.

COME AFTER DARK, THE RE-ANIMATING SPIRIT IS SET LOOSE, EAGER FOR ITS EXERCISE, AND GREEN ARC-LIGHT FLASHES ON WALLS OF DAMP BASALT.

A SINE WAVE SHIMMERS, CONDENSES INTO A JAGGED SIZZLE, THEN STRETCHES IN A FUNNEL OF LUMINOUS THREADS TOWARDS THE VAULTED SHADOWS ABOVE.

HOW QUICKLY THIS DEMON LEARNS, CAVORTING IN ITS CHALK CIRCLE.

IT WILL NOT ABIDE FOR LONG IN THIS PLACE.

REARED UPON THEIR HIND LEGS, MONITORS SWAY GENTLY IN THE DUSK WINDS. HIGH ABOVE, TETHERED TO SPARS OF CRYSTAL, DWARF PTERANODONS CLACK DROWSILY TO EACH OTHER, SETTLING DOWN FOR THE DARK, AND WITH THEIR SPARSE BONE PERCUSSION THE EVENING IS MADE PERFECT, MADE COMPLETE.

FILLED WITH SENTIMENTS THAT HAVE NO NAMES, MEDPHYL HOLDS HIS MASTER AND KNOWS THAT THIS IS THE LAST NIGHT.

YOU... YOU WILL BE LEAVING SOON?

YES, I AM CONFIDENT OF MY ABILITY... TO MODIFY MY WAVELENGTH... ASSURED THAT THE EARTH... WILL ONCE AGAIN *ACCEPT* ME...

I AM ANXIOUS... TO *RETURN* THERE...

I CANNOT... THANK YOU ENOUGH... FOR *AIDING* ME SO... WHEN I HAVE BROUGHT YOU... ONLY TROUBLE...

NO, NOT TROUBLE. YOU MUST NOT THINK THAT...

YOU ARE... TOO FORGIVING. I SHALL IMPOSE... UPON YOU NO FURTHER. GOODBYE... MY FRIEND.

WAIT! YOU HAVE GIVEN ME MORE THAN YOU CAN POSSIBLY *KNOW.* YOU'VE GIVEN ME A CHANCE TO COME TO TERMS WITH MY GRIEF.

A CHANCE TO SAY GOODBYE TO...

JOTHRA?

FROM THEIR SEPARATE WINDOWS, DISMA AND LOCLISS WATCH THE EMERALD SHOOTING STAR ASCEND.

ELSEWHERE, SHURLO WANTS TO PAINT IT, TO CAPTURE ITS LONELINESS.

IMREL, PAUSING IN MID SERMON, TAKES IT FOR A SIGN.

AND, IN THE LIZARD GARDENS, GREAT MEDPHYL WEEPS, AND THE WEEPING IS GOOD. FROM J586 A BOLT OF GREEK FIRE CRACKLES INTO THE VOID, GOING AWAY...

20

GOING HOME.

IT'S GOOD OF YOU TO HELP ME GET THIS ACID RAIN REPORT TOGETHER, AFTER... A-AFTER ALL THE WEIRDNESS THE OTHER WEEK I FIGURED MAYBE YOU'D STEER CLEAR...

≶ THPPFT ≷

OH, HEY, NO. NO WAY!

I MEAN, I GUESS IT DID FREAK ME OUT, SORT OF, BUT HEY, I KNOW YOU WERE INTO SOME STRANGE SPACES ALL ALONG.

≶ THPPFT ≷ YOU WANT SOME OF THIS?

NO, NO THANKS, I DON'T.

THAT'S COOL. Y'KNOW, IT'S A REAL TRIP WORKING WITH YOU ON THIS. I KNOW I HAVEN'T KNOWN YOU LONG, BUT...

GENG·GLANG

UH OH, CHESTER, I DON'T KNOW WHO THAT IS, BUT HIDE THAT STUFF WHILE I ANSWER IT.

THIS IS LOUISIANA, REMEMBER.

ABIGAIL CABLE? DO I HAVE THE RIGHT ADDRESS?

UH, YES, YES I'M ABBY CABLE, YOU'RE...?

STRANGE.

ADAM STRANGE.

I'VE GOT A MESSAGE FOR YOU, FROM YOUR LOVER, THE SWAMP CREATURE. HE TOLD ME TO TELL YOU HE'S ALIVE AND...

WHAAT? ALEC SAID THIS? OH GOD!

WHOA! SLOW DOWN. WHAT IS ALL THIS?

21

WELL, THE COMPLETE MESSAGE I WAS ASKED TO GIVE MS. CABLE IS THAT SWAMP THING IS STILL ALIVE AND PROMISES TO RETURN AS SOON AS HE CAN.

OH, THIS IS *WONDERFUL.* I CAN'T *BELIEVE* IT. WHERE *IS* HE?

I MET HIM ON THE PLANET *RANN* IN THE *CENTAURI* SYSTEM, BUT HE WAS HEADING ON TO *J586,* NEAR *MINRAUD.*

AFTER THAT, ALL BEING WELL, HE MAY BE COMING *HOME.*

HE HELPED AVERT A FAMINE, AND I SAID I'D DELIVER HIS MESSAGE AS *REPAYMENT.*

I TRAVEL BACK AND FORTH BETWEEN RANN AND THIS PLANET ON A *ZETA BEAM* QUITE REGULARLY, SO YOU SEE IT'S REALLY NO TROUBLE...

NO? WELL YOU JUST CALL UP *SCOTTY* ON YOUR *COMMUNICATOR* AND TELL HIM TO *ZETA BEAM* YOU THE HELL *OUT* OF HERE, YOU GODDAMNED LUNATIC!

BUT...

COME ON, MAN, I THINK MAYBE YOU BETTER SPLIT.

BUT YOU DON'T *UNDERSTAND.* I'VE BEEN DOING THIS FOR *YEARS* NOW. THERE'S A FLASH OF *LIGHT,* AND I'M ON ANOTHER *PLANET.*

YEAH...

YEAH, I SOMETIMES GET THAT.

NEXT: WAVELENGTH

22

CHAPTER 6

"THEY WERE *LOVERS,* SIRE...

"*LOVERS* IN THE PLACE OF *GIANTS.*

"I VISITED THEM OFTEN IN THEIR *BRIDAL SUITE,* AND WAS WITNESS TO THE SPECTACLE OF THEIR *FROZEN PASSION.*

"THERE TO PONDER THE LESSONS OF *FUTILITY* ON DISPLAY, SCULPTED BY THE *LIVING FLESH* OF BEINGS THE *SIZE OF STAR CLUSTERS.*

"POOR *CELESTIALS,* LIKE *OURSELVES,* WHO *DARED* ATTEMPT THAT WHICH I ONCE THOUGHT *UNATTAINABLE...*

"*CONDEMNED* TO DRIFT IN ETERNAL HUMILIATING *SEPARATION...*

"FROM EACH OTHER...

"...AND FROM THE *SOURCE.*"

"AND SO, SIRE, I FOUND MY WAY BACK TO THE LAST SIGNPOST ON THE FRINGES OF THE KNOWN UNIVERSE, THE PROMETHIAN GALAXY...

"...WHERE DWELLS THE CURSE OF METRON."

I SHOULD HAVE KNOWN.

ANOTHER RIVULET OF REALITY THAT MY MOBIUS CHAIR HAS OPENED TO ME, ONLY LEADING BACK...BACK TO THE SOURCE.

THE ONE CONSTANT IN A UNIVERSE OF CHANGE-- IT REMAINS AS EVER, SERENE, OMNIPOTENT, ALL-WISE... THE ULTIMATE MYSTERY HIDDEN BEHIND THE FINAL BARRIER.

THESE POOR CREATURES WERE ONCE SEARCHERS, LIKE MYSELF. THEY TRIED TO ENLARGE THEIR ATOMIC STRUCTURES IN HOPES OF ENGULFING THE FINAL BARRIER...

HOW SAD WHEN HEARTS THAT ONCE LIVED ONLY FOR EACH OTHER TAKE A MILLION YEARS TO FEEL A SINGLE BEAT.

THEY CRY OUT THAT ALL HOPE OF UNVEILING THE SOURCE IS FOLLY...

IF THAT IS TRUE, THEN METRON'S WHOLE LIFE IS FOLLY...

AND PERHAPS IT IS TIME HE TOOK HIS PLACE AMONG THE OTHER FAILURES...

2

"IT WAS A *SIGNAL*, SIRE... SO PATHETICALLY FAINT THAT EVEN MY *WONDROUS MOBIUS CHAIR* COULD BARELY FOLLOW IT..."

PING

PING

PING

PING

PING

Ping

"STRANGER STILL, IT SEEMED TO BE EMANATING FROM THE SHOULDER HARNESS OF ONE OF THE *FROZEN COLOSSI.*"

"ALWAYS CURIOUS WHEN CONFRONTED WITH UNEXPLAINED PHENOMENA, I DECIDED TO INVESTIGATE..."

PING

PING

PING

PING

I'M SURE THE *MADAME* WILL PARDON THIS INTRUSION IN THE NAME OF SCIENCE.

AMAZING.

THINGS ARE *GROWING* IN HERE... BIZARRE FLORA THAT I'VE NEVER ENCOUNTERED BEFORE, SOMEHOW TENACIOUSLY CLINGING TO LIFE IN THE ARTIFICIAL ENVIRONMENT OF HER *SPACESUIT.*

JUST A FEW SAMPLES FOR FURTHER STUDY, THEN I'LL TRACK DOWN THIS MYSTERIOUS *SIGNAL...*

I'LL BE DAMNED IF IT DOESN'T SOUND ALMOST... *FAMILIAR.*

PING

PING

PING

PING

PING

PING

BY *HIGHFATHER'S* BEARD -- IT'S A *MOTHER BOX...* SWOLLEN TO THE SIZE OF A SMALL MOON!

④

"OF COURSE, SIRE, YOU KNOW BETTER THAN ANYONE WHAT IT TOOK TO OBTAIN THE ORIGINAL X-ELEMENT!

"AND I... I HAD NOTHING BUT TIME TO PONDER THE PRICE OF REPLACING IT...

PING

"THE HUMOR OF THE SITUATION IS THAT I STILL MIGHT BE OUT THERE BUT FOR THAT WRETCHED MOTHER BOX.

"DEEPLY INTO ONE WITH NATURE, SHE HAD FOUND SOMETHING PASSING BY IN THE VOID, AND HAD MANAGED TO PULL IT IN...

PING PIING

PING! PING PING PING PING PING Pir

PING PING! PING!

"SOMETHING THAT FIRST APPEARED AS A SELF-CONTAINED FIELD OF PURE ELECTROMAGNETIC ENERGY!

"IT DANCED 'ROUND ME LIKE A WHIRLING DERVISH, UNTIL SUDDENLY, AS A STARVING MAN SMELLING FOOD, IT LEAPT TOWARDS MY INERT MOBIUS CHAIR...

"THERE TO GAIN A MIRACULOUS FOOTHOLD ON THE PHYSICAL PLANE.

"BUT MOST ASTONISHING OF ALL, WAS WHAT FORMED AND STOOD BEFORE ME WAS NEITHER MAN, NOR MACHINE, NOR PURE ENERGY FORM..."

SHLORP

PLUP SQUESH

FLARP

7

"...HE WAS A VEGETABLE."

WAVELENGTH

Rick Veitch
GUEST WRITER / PENCILER

Alfredo Alcala
INKER

Tatjana Wood
colorist

John Costanza
letterer

Karen Berger
EDITOR

CREATED BY LEN WEIN and BERNI WRIGHTSON

8

FEAR NOT. I MEAN YOU...NO HARM. JUST TELL ME...WHERE I AM...*THIS* TIME.

ASK *HER*. SHE'S THE ONE WHO BROUGHT YOU HERE.

PERSONALLY, I WAS HOPING FOR SOMETHING A LITTLE MORE *GODLIKE*...

PING

THIS...WAS THE COMFORTING VOICE... THAT CALLED TO ME...IN THE VOID? IT IS STRANGE...THAT YOU WOULD ADDRESS...A MACHINE...AS *HER*.

AND YET...I FEEL IT *TOO*. THAT SOMEHOW... SHE IS *ALIVE*.

PING

ALIVE...AND TRYING... TO *TELL* ME SOMETHING...

...EVERYTHING... PING

PING PING PING

PING PING PING

OH, SHE'LL *NAG* YOUR EAR OFF IF YOU LET HER.

SHE TELLS ME... SHE BROUGHT ME *HERE*... BECAUSE *YOU* WISH TO GO *THERE*...INTO WHAT SHE CALLS...THE *SOURCE*.

WRONG! WHAT I NEED NOW IS *TRANSPORT* FOR MYSELF AND MY EQUIPMENT TO A PLACE CALLED *APOKOLIPS*.

NO, YOUR DESTINY...IS *THERE*... WITHIN THE CENTER... OF *EVERYTHING*.

AND NOW... THAT I'VE SEEN IT...SO IS *MINE*.

PIIING!

9

HRRRUMPH! AND WHAT *OTHER* FANTASIES HAS THIS... THIS *CALCULATOR* INFORMED YOU OF?

THAT SHE AND I...WORKING *TOGETHER*...CAN TAKE YOU INTO THE *SOURCE* AND BACK.

IT IS NOT FOR ONE SUCH AS *I* TO RIDE UNGAINLY IN THE ARMS OF SOME *MONSTROSITY*.

WHEN METRON CONQUERS THE FINAL *BARRIER*, HE SHALL DO SO AS THE *CELESTIAL* HE IS... SEATED IN HIS *WONDROUS MOBIUS CHAIR*.

SOME OF THE MOST DIFFICULT LESSONS...IN MY JOURNEYS...HAVE CONCERNED... POWER AND EGO.

I'VE LEARNED IT IS NOT *WISE*... TO LET *SELF IMAGE*... GET IN THE WAY OF *UNDERSTANDING*.

PING PING

IF YOU UNDERSTOOD WHAT IT MEANT TO BE A GOD, YOU'D KNOW I HAVE NO *CHOICE*.

THEN *MY* CHOICE...IS TO *COOPERATE*... WITH *DESTINY*... AND BECOME YOUR ...*VEHICLE*.

PING
SLIP
PING
PLOOP
PING
FRUP
PING
SHLAK
PING

HA! AN *ELEGANT* SOLUTION FOR SUCH A *LOWER LIFE FORM*.

PERHAPS I *WILL* CONSENT TO ACCOMPANY YOU, AS YOUR *PILOT* OF COURSE.

OF COURSE...

PING

ALTHOUGH I HAVE NEVER MOVED MY *PHYSICAL BODY*... THROUGH THE *VOID*...

MOTHER BOX SAYS THAT *SHE*... CAN MAKE IT POSSIBLE.

JUST AS SHE PROVIDES...THE *BOOST* WE NEED... TO CLEAR THE GRAVITY... OF THIS *PROMETHIAN GIANT*.

10

"AND SO, SIRE, WE QUICKLY LEFT THE REALM OF FROZEN FAILURES BEHIND, ON A COLLISION COURSE WITH THE FINAL BARRIER."

TELL ME, OH VEGETABLE... BY WHAT *METHOD* DO YOU INTEND TO *TRANSCEND* THE BARRIER?

MOTHER BOX INDICATES... THAT *ALL* EXISTENCE... IS *PURELY* VIBRATIONAL... AT THE MOST BASIC LEVEL.

AND THAT TO EXPLORE...AREAS *BEYOND* OUR OWN ...ONE NEEDS TO ONLY OSCILLATE AT *OTHER* FREQUENCIES.

IT IS... MOTHER BOX THAT *TRULY*... UNDER-STANDS.

SHE MAKES IT SO *EASY*...TO PLAY *SUBTLE* VARIATIONS... UPON THE *HARMONIC SCALE* ...OF NATURE.

I HAVE BEEN DOING IT...CRUDELY...FOR A *LONG* TIME.

ONLY *NOW*... AM I BEGINNING TO FATHOM...JUST HOW *FAR*... IT MIGHT TAKE ME.

I HAVE RECENTLY COME...FROM A PLACE WHERE I LEARNED...HOW TO *CONTROL*... THE *FREQUENCY* OF MY *ELECTRO-MAGNETIC FIELD.*

AND THIS IS SOMETHING YOU ARE FAMILIAR WITH?

I *RECOGNIZE*... THIS LEVEL.

IT WOULD BE...*GREEN* IF THERE WERE A...PLANETARY *ECOSYSTEM*... NEARBY IN THE *PHYSICAL REALM.*

AND HERE WOULD EXIST... THE *DOMAIN OF SOULS*...WERE THERE A RACE OF SENTIENT BEINGS... TO MAKE IT THEIR *PARADISE.*

11

"BUT FIRST, THERE WAS A BIT OF UNPLEASANTNESS THAT HAD TO BE DEALT WITH..."

METRON... IS *THAT*... THE SOURCE?

NOT *LIKELY!* IT'S A *TRANSMUTER*-- THEY'RE POSTED ALL ALONG THE *FRINGES* OF REALITY...

THEY WORK THE DENSE *COMPOST* OF CREATION INTO GLOBULES OF *HIGHER MATTER* TO BE FED BACK INTO THE GREAT SCHEME OF THINGS.

THEY ARE *WELL KNOWN* TO THOSE WHO RIDE THE DIMENSIONAL WAVES.

AMAZING... I COULD NEVER IMAGINE...THAT SO MUCH... PURE CREATIVE ENERGY... COULD BE FOCUSED... IN ONE PLACE.

IT ONLY MEANS WE'VE TRAVELLED IN THE *WRONG* DIRECTION!

THE SOURCE IS THE *CENTER* OF EVERYTHING. THEREFORE, IT MUST BE AT THE *HIGHEST* PART OF THE SPECTRUM.

HMMM... I WOULD HAVE THOUGHT... JUST THE *OPPOSITE.*

WATCH OUT! HE'S LOOKING THIS WAY!

HE'S *SENSED* US! IF HE FIXES HIS GAZE ON US THEN *WE TOO* SHALL *SUFFER TRANSMUTATION!*

YOU'VE GOT TO *INCREASE* THE *VIBRATION RATE*-- PROPEL US *OUT* OF HERE AND INTO THE *SOURCE! NOW!*

13

"AS I COME NOW TO THE INEFFABLE CLIMAX OF MY STORY, MY DESPAIR AS A NARRATOR BEGINS. TO DESCRIBE THE SOURCE... HOW DOES ONE CONVEY THE ACT OF SEEING ALL OF INFINITY WITHIN ONE GIGANTIC INSTANT? TO DRINK IN BILLIONS OF ACTIONS, THE TOTALITY OF EVERYTHING, OBSERVED FROM EVERY POINT IN THE UNIVERSE, ALL IN LESS TIME THAN IT TAKES TO DRAW A SINGLE BREATH. EVEN MY GREAT INTELLECT WAS OVERWHELMED BY IT, SIRE. WHAT MY EYES SAW WAS SIMULTANEOUS AND OCCUPYING THE SAME POINT, SO I CAN ONLY ACCOUNT FOR WHAT WONDERS I WAS ABLE TO FOCUS ON AND REMEMBER IN THAT TIDAL WAVE OF INFORMATION..."

"AND I SAW IT ALL, SIRE, FROM THE GREAT GALACTIC STRUCTURES...

"TO THE LOWLIEST SWARMS OF MICROBES...

"I SAW THEM FROM EVERY ANGLE...

"I SAW THE COMETS SOWING SEEDS OF LIFE THROUGHOUT EMERGING STAR SYSTEMS...

"AND THEN I SAW THAT LIFE, FULLY EVOLVED A BILLION YEARS LATER, GRAZING ON THE FERTILE PLAINS OF NUMBERLESS PLANETS...

"I SAW THE GODS, IN THEIR 'FINAL' CONFLICTS, TEARING THEIR MYTHICAL WORLDS ASUNDER IN ORGY AFTER MEANINGLESS ORGY OF VIOLENCE...

"ONE OF THEM WAS MY OWN FATHER.

"I SAW A STREET, IN THE HEART OF CHICAGO; LOOKED IN ALL THE WINDOWS, LOOKED OUT ALL THE WINDOWS, SAW ALL THE STREETS ON EARTH, ON ALL THE EARTHS.

"I WITNESSED A MULTITUDE OF UNIVERSES COLLAPSING UPON EACH OTHER, ATTEMPTING UNIFICATION INTO A SINGLE COHERENT COSMOLOGY...

"...LEAVING INNUMERABLE SENTIENT BEINGS UNAWARE OF WHAT HAPPENED...LIVING THEIR LIVES AS IF ALL WERE NORMAL...

"...AS IF THE GREAT WHEEL OF CREATION HADN'T BEEN THROWN CRAZILY OUT OF BALANCE...

15

"I SMELT RANCID GREASE DRIPPING ON A STOVETOP COUNTER..."

"...AND WONDERED AT THE BEAUTY OF THE TAJ MAHAL..."

"I FLEW WITH PTERO-DACTYLS, WINGS BEATING FURIOUSLY IN AN ATTEMPT TO OUTRACE EXTINCTION..."

"I SAW THE SEASONS OF THE YEAR UNFOLD-ING, ALL THE SEASONS OF ALL THE YEARS..."

"A BABY KITTEN, SUFFERING DISTEMPER..."

"ALL THE PAWNS MOVED IN ALL THE GAMES EVER PLAYED..."

"A PEACOCK, SPREAD-ING HIS FEATHERS, REVEALING THE GAZE OF A HUNDRED JEWELED EYES..."

"I SAW THE HEEL OF A SHOE, CRUSHING A DELICATE FLOWER..."

"...THE MANIA AND DELUSIONS THAT ACCOMPANY ALL CIVILIZATIONS."

"I WATCHED THE ELEMENTS BEING FORMED WITHIN THE CRUCIBLES OF THE STARS..."

"...THE GASES THAT BREW IN THE CLOSED SYSTEMS OF THE PLANETS..."

" THE OMENS THAT AUGUR ALL FUTURE ACTS..."

"...A GAMBLER'S DISCARDS."

"I SAW TIME, NOT AS A LINEAR PROGRES-SION OF EVENTS, BUT AS A SINGLE HARMON-IC EXPLOSION..."

"I SAW A PEBBLE, TOSSED INTO A POND, RIPPLING OUT IN PERFECT CONCENTRIC PATTERNS..."

"I FOLLOWED THE SPOOR OF THE YETI..."

"I LIFTED THE COLUMNS OF THE ACROPOLIS IN FEAR AND HONOR OF THE GODS..."

"I KNEW THE HUBRIS OF OUR ANCESTORS AS THEY LOOKED DOWN ON THESE OFFERINGS..."

"I SAW A GREAT SHIP, ITS RUDDER GONE, SIDES SPLIT ASUNDER BY A TREACHEROUS REEF..."

"I WAS THE REEF, A COMPLETE ECOSYSTEM WELCOMING THE SHIP'S CREW TO MY WATERY BOSOM..."

"I FELT THE MOTHER BOX, AND UNDERSTOOD HER COMMUNION WITH NATURE..."

"...HER CONNECTION TO THE VEGETABLE..."

"AND HIS CONNECTION TO EARTH."

"I SAW HIS FACE SCREAMING AS THE MADNESS OVERCAME HIM..."

"I SAW MY FACE..."

17

"I SAW YOUR FACE, SIRE."

HAH!

BY MY BROW, METRON, YOU ACADEMIC CHICKEN-- YOU'VE NOT ENTERED THE SOURCE AT ALL! THAT TRANSMUTER HOODWINKED YOU WITH AN ALEPH!

ALEPHS ARE POINTS FROM WHICH ONE CAN OBSERVE ALL OTHER POINTS IN TIME AND SPACE. THEY ARE CONSIDERED PARLOR TRICKS TO ANY SORCERER WORTHY OF HIS TRADE.

YOU'VE SPENT TOO MUCH TIME TRYING TO UNRAVEL THE PHYSICS OF REALITY, METRON, AND NOT PAID ENOUGH ATTENTION TO CABAL. LET ME WARN YOU-- THERE SHALL BE NO ROOM FOR INTELLECTUALS IN THIS UNIVERSE WHEN DARKSEID SOLVES THE ANTI-LIFE EQUATION.

A-AN ALEPH? THEN...THE SOURCE RETAINS ITS MYSTERY...AND I'VE NOTHING TO BARTER, SIRE... NOTHING I CAN OFFER IN TRADE FOR MORE OF THE X-ELEMENT...

NO HOPE OF REGAINING MY REPUTATION THROUGH THE POWER OF MY MOBIUS CHAIR...

18

DESPAIR NOT, METRON.

I HAVE NEED OF *OTHER* TYPES OF KNOWLEDGE... ANYTHING THAT MIGHT *ASSIST* WITH THE COMPUTATION OF THE *ANTI-LIFE EQUATION...*

BUT *WHAT*, SIRE? I'VE TOLD YOU EVERYTHING.

WELL, THIS *VEGETABLE* INTERESTS ME. HOW CAME SUCH A BEING INTO EXISTENCE? WHO IS HE?

A LEGEND PERHAPS?

WELL, HE *DID* COME FROM EARTH ORIGINALLY...

BEFORE HIS *AURA* DEPARTED FOR EARTH HE SPOKE OF HIS MANY ENEMIES THERE... ACCOUNTS THAT HAD TO BE SETTLED... A *WOMAN* HE FANCIED.

IN TRUTH, HE WAS A *STRANGE* BEING, FILLED WITH THE KIND OF LONGINGS ONE ASSOCIATES WITH *HUMANKIND.*

I SENSED HE CARRIED GREAT POWER WITHIN HIM, AN ELEMENTAL POWER THAT OPERATED PERHAPS ON A PLANETARY SCALE.

YET YOU SAY HE WENT *MAD*...

TELL ME, WHAT WOULD *CAUSE* ONE SO POWERFUL TO LOSE HIS SANITY SO QUICKLY...

...SO EFFICIENTLY?

IT WAS WHAT HE *SAW* WHEN WE ENTERED THE *ALEPH*, SIRE.

IN FACT, MOTHER BOX HAD TO *REMOVE* ALL HIS *MEMORIES* OF THE EXPERIENCE IN ORDER FOR HIM TO *FUNCTION* WELL ENOUGH TO RETURN US TO NORMAL REALITY.

THEN SHE WOULD HAVE A *RECORD* OF WHAT THE VEGETABLE SAW AND FELT WHILE WITHIN THE ALEPH?

I SUPPOSE SHE WOULD, SIRE.

PING

THEN I WOULD *REVIEW* THIS RECORD.

OF *COURSE*, SIRE!

IT-IT'S JUST THAT MOTHER BOX *FEARS* YOU SO -- SHE DOESN'T WANT TO TELL YOU *ANYTHING.*

P-PERHAPS IF I BYPASS HER EMOTIONAL CIRCUITS...

PING
PING
PING
PING
PING
PING
PING

19

"THE FUTURE... OUR FUTURE... TOGETHER?"

"OH, PLEASE..."

"EMBRACING YOU? YOUR FULL LIPS BRUSHING MY OWN...?"

"IN THE SWAMP... FREE FROM ALL PRYING...?"

"IS IT POSSIBLE?"

"A WHITE HAND... SLOWLY TURNING GREEN..."

"I'M DIVING... FOR PEARLS IN AN OCEAN OF EMERALD... LIGHT."

"I SEE YOU LOST... BUT HAPPY... LAUGHING... THERE IS NO DANGER..."

"NOTHING TO FEAR..."

"THE WHITE HAND... NOW EMERALD... GRASPING THE YOUNG SHOOT..."

"CONSTANTINE...?"

"A CARNIVOROUS PLANT... THE SIZE OF... A FOOTBALL STADIUM..."

"...ABBY, WHAT ARE YOU AND CONSTANTINE...?"

"THE PARLIAMENT OF TREES... DEMANDING..."

"ABBY...?"

"BUT I LOVE..."

"A MAN... BURNING... RUNNING FOR THE SWAMPS."

"BURNING..."

"A PARCHED... AND CHALKY HAND... NOW GREEN... PULLING THE SHOOT... OUT BY THE ROOTS..."

"ANOTHER MAN BURNS..."

"ABBY..."

"THE GREEN DIMENSION... WITHERING... ROTTING... DROPPING AWAY PIECEMEAL."

"ABBY, YOUR LOVE..."

"A WITCH DOCTOR... DEEP IN THE NEW GUINEA RAIN FOREST... GRINDING POWDERS IN A CEREMONIAL BOWL..."

"YOUR LOVE..."

"MORE BURNING... A WOMAN, SCREAMING..."

"YOUR LOVE WAS ALL..."

"MY NAME IS ALEC OLSEN... NO! HOLLAND..."

"YOUR LOVE WAS ALL THAT KEPT ME..."

"THE BURNING... NO-- PLEASE DON'T LET ME..."

"ALL THAT KEPT ME..."

"STOP THE BURNING."

"ALL THAT KEPT ME SANE..."

PING! PING! PING! PING! PING! PING!

PING! PING!

DIVING ACROSS A GALAXY, DOWN, DOWN, THROUGH STARS AND STARS AND STARS AND FINALLY CLOUDS, THE ROLLING LAND-OCEAN BELOW APPROACHING FAST AS A TRAIN, BECOMING BIGGER, BECOMING EVERYTHING UNTIL HE BREAKS, NO, SHATTERS THE SURFACE, A SOLID SPLASH...

...PENETRATING LUKEWARM TOPSOIL, PAST THE WORM-SHOALS, SHIMMERING, WRITHING IN THE SHALLOWS, PLUNGING DEEPER, THROUGH THE THRILLING COLD STREAMS OF THE CLAYBEDS AND OH, OH THE FEELING AND HE IS HOME...

FINALLY, HOME.

ABOVE GREAT GEOLOGIC WAVES OF EARTH AND ROCK RACE IMPERCEPTIBLY CROSS-CONTINENT TO BREAK, PERHAPS, A MILLION YEARS FROM NOW, AGAINST THE SEA.

ABOVE, THE TREESTUMPS RADIATE PALE TENDRILS, ROTTEN STARS BENEATH WHICH SKELETONS OF CATS AND HORSES HANG SUSPENDED IN THE STEAD OF CLOUDS. THE COAL SEAM IS A REEF OF JET, ITS PLATES PRECARIOUSLY STACKED, LIKE DIRTY DISHES, AND, BELOW THAT, MONSTERS, MONSTERS AND THEIR FOOTPRINTS BEFORE MILES OF STONE AND ULTIMATELY FIRE.

THE BURIED RIVERBED'S A PEBBLE RIBBON WHERE THE FISHBONES HOVER, DREAMING OF THEIR FORMER LIVES, AND THERE, AMONGST THE KEELS OF ROCKS, HE THINKS OF HER, THE IMPRINT OF THEIR LAST EMBRACE A CHERISHED BRUISE UPON HIS SPIRIT, PURPLE STILL AND TENDER DESPITE ALL THE LONG AND HOLLOW MONTHS ALONE.

THEY'D RUN TOWARDS EACH OTHER, KISSED, EMBRACED, THEN HE HAD BURNED AS IF THE ARC-FLASH OF THEIR CONTACT HAD TRANS-FORMED HIM INTO A THING OF ASH, INCINERATED BY HIS LOVE, BY HIS DESIRE, CONDEMNED TO A MAD AFTERLIFE BEYOND THE FURTHER STARS...

AMONGST THE KEELS OF ROCKS HE THINKS OF HER, AND OF THE MEN WHO'D KEPT HER FROM HIM...

OF A LOVE TOO LONG UNCONSUMMATED AND UNFINISHED WARS.

LOOSE ENDS (REPRISE)

ALAN MOORE · **RICK VEITCH & ALFREDO ALCALA** · **KAREN BERGER**
WRITER · ARTISTS · EDITOR

TATJANA WOOD · **JOHN COSTANZA**
colorist · letterer

3

THERE'S A GARDEN WHERE ILLNESSES GROW, RIPENING GRADUALLY TOWARDS RECOVERY OR DEATH...

THE CIRCLING LIGHTS OF AN AMBULANCE GROVE SCATTER RED BLOSSOM ON THE WET AND TWINKLING GRAVEL AT HER FEET AS SHE APPROACHES.

KEEP CLEAR EMERGENCY HICLES ONLY

TERREBONNE PARISH GENERAL HOSPITAL

INSIDE, THE ACOUSTICS CHANGE, BECOMING HUSHED AND INFLATED, FILLED WITH WHISPERING DISTANCES WHERE COMFORTINGS AND CONDOLENCES MERGE INTO A SYMPATHETIC MURMUR OF FARAWAY RUSHES.

IN CASUALTY RECEPTION, POPPIES GROW UPON GAUZE, FIRST BLOOMS OF A CATASTROPHIC SPRING.

A CHLOROFORM-SCENTED BREEZE MOVES THROUGH THE FORMALDE-HYDE TREES, BEARS THE MEASURED AND PLAINTIVE EVEN-SONG OF THE HEART-MONITORS TO HER AS SHE WALKS PAST THE WARDS WITH THEIR COTS IN CORNFIELD ROWS, AWAITING HARVEST...

...FINALLY REACHING THE CELLAR-CULTURES, STILL AND LIGHT-STARVED IN THEIR BEDS, PALE FLESH SUBTLY LUMINOUS LIKE THAT OF MUSHROOMS.

ON HER EARLIEST VISITS SHE'D TRIED TO PROVOKE SOME RESPONSE. IF HE SPOKE NOW, SHE'D ALMOST BE FRIGHTENED.

DEAD IN ALL BUT NAME, WANDERING LOST SOMEWHERE AMONGST THE STEEP GREEN HILLS SKETCHED ON HIS EEG SCREEN.

HIS BODY'S THE GRAVE OF HIS MIND, ROOTED THERE, TRANSLUCENT STALKS RISE FROM VEIN AND NOSTRIL INTO GLASS FLOWERS CONTAINING GLUCOSE TO LURE BEES.

IF TOUCHED, THEY CHIME, BRIEF AND MELANCHOLY.

GENG·GLANG

9:34

GENGA
GENG
GLANG

UH, HI. IT'S *LIZ*, RIGHT?
LIZ *TREMAYNE*?

A-ALL
RIGHT.

ALL
RIGHT,
I'M JUST
COMING.

I'M CHESTER
WILLIAMS. I
WORK WITH
ABBY'S
ENVIRONMENTAL
GROUP AND I
TOLD HER I'D
COME BY THIS
EVENING. IS
SHE *HOME?*

UH, NO. NO, SHE'S
NOT. YOU BETTER
COME IN...

OKAY, THANKS.
SAY, THAT *CAR*
SHE HIRED LAST
WEEK, DID SHE
TAKE IT *BACK?*
I DIDN'T SEE IT
OUTSIDE...

NO, SHE...SHE DROVE IT TO
THE HOSPITAL, VISITING
MATT, HER HUSBAND...

OH, RIGHT,
THE GUY WHO HAD THE
ACCIDENT. Y'KNOW, SHE'S
ONE TOGETHER LADY. ALL
THE *BUMMERS* IN HER
LIFE AND SHE CARRIES *ON,*
WORKING WITH THE *ECO*
GROUP, TAKING CARE
OF *YOU...*

UH, NO
OFFENSE.

5

OH NO, NO, IT'S OKAY. SHE HELPS ME SO MUCH, I KNOW.

YOU MUST THINK I'M PATHETIC.

YOU'RE RIGHT.

I DON'T HELP OUT ENOUGH, I'M USELESS WITH...

HEY! SLOW DOWN!

YOU'RE SOMEBODY WHO GOT *HEAD TRIPPED* REAL BAD, IS ALL. IT *HAPPENS.* I DON'T THINK YOU'RE PATHETIC.

Y-YOU DON'T?

NO WAY, YOU'RE BEAUTIFUL. YOU JUST HAVE TO MELLOW *OUT* A LITTLE.

ANYWAY, ABBY'S AT THE *HOSPITAL.* I OUGHTA TRUCK ON OVER THERE TO *MEET* HER.

YOU TAKE IT EASY, OKAY?

IN THE BATHROOM MIRROR SHE HAS A PLAIN WOMAN'S HAIR; A STAIN ON HER ROBE WHERE SHE SPILLED HER CEREAL...

TAKING ONE OF ABBY'S SUMMER DRESSES FROM THE CLOSET, SHE HOLDS IT FLAT TO HER BODY BEFORE REPLACING IT.

HEART HAMMERING, SHE RUNS A BATH, FOUR INCHES DEEP, AND SUMMONS THE COURAGE TO SIT. RECKLESSLY, SHE'S USED TOO MUCH BATH GELÉE. AS THE FOAM-DRIFT PILES AGAINST HER BACK SHE WONDERS IF YOU CAN DROWN IN BUBBLES, BUT DOES NOT SCREAM.

BEAUTIFUL.

HE SAID BEAUTIFUL.

SHE'S NO DOG.

PRESSING HER DOORBELL, FOLEY'S SHOULDER HURTS: GODDAMN RECOIL, ROCKET LAUNCHER IN GOTHAM. HE HOPES IT WON'T SPOIL TONIGHT.

THREE DOLLARS BLOWN ON FLOWERS, WONDERING IF SHE'LL STILL LOOK GOOD SOBER, BUT THEN SHE'S THERE, HOT STEAM FOGGING ICED GLASS BEHIND HER, AND HEY...

HEY, SHE'S NO DOG.

HI, ANGEL. HERE I *AM*, RIGHT ON *TIME*. I, UH, I GOTCHA THIS LITTLE BUNCH OF FLOWERS, I KNOW THEY AIN'T MUCH...

GUS, THEY'RE *FANTASTIC*. THEY MUST HAVE COST A *FORTUNE!*

HERE... YOU PUT 'EM IN *WATER* AND...

HERE, GIVE THEM TO ME.

HMM, GUESS YOU *DO* GET A PRETTY BIG BUNCH. LOOKED SMALLER IN THE *STORE*.

HELL, GOT IT SNAGGED ON MY SUIT HERE. EXCUSE ME...

OH *CAREFUL*, DON'T TEAR THE *JACKET*...

NO, NO, I WON'T, I'M JUST... GODDAMN, THIS HAS GOT LOOSE BRIARS ALL OVER IT! I OUGHTA COMPLAIN TO... OWW.

GUS, YOU'RE GETTING ALL TANGLED. LET ME...

NO, YOU'LL CATCH IT ALL OVER YOUR *ROBE* AND... HEY!

IS THERE SOME *ANIMAL* ALIVE IN THIS? IT JUST *MOVED!*

GUS, DON'T *PANIC*, IT'S...

I'M *NOT* PANICKING, YOU STUPID *SLUT!* THIS MOTHER JUST *AAAA!*

GUS?

AAA, WHAT THE HELL?

JESUS, IT'S... AAAAAAGH! GET IT *OFF!* GET IT *OFF* ME, IT'S... AAK.

GUS, *DON'T!* YOU'RE *FRIGHTENING* ME!

7

THERE'D BEEN HORROR AND OLD-STYLE DEAN MARTIN ROMANCE; MONSTERS AND CHOCOLATES AND BLOOD AND BOUQUETS.

SO MUCH BETWEEN THEM, SO MUCH TO UNDERSTAND: HE'D HELPED HER, MADE LOVE TO HER, MARRIED HER, ALMOST DESTROYED HER...

HER HUSBAND.

THE VEGETABLE.

HIS BREAST RISES, AND FALLS.

THE TIDES OF BREATH SURGING THROUGH US ALL, MAKING US MERE CHANNELS FOR ITS PHANTOM OCEANS, THOSE TIDES ARE SPENT BUT LIMPLY ON THE SHORES OF THE STAGNANT INLET HE'S BECOME...

LAP.

LAP.

LAP.

SHE TRIES TO CLEARLY PICTURE THEIR RELATIONSHIP, ENCLOSE IT IN A FRAME, MAKE IT COHERENT, BUT THERE'S TOO MUCH DRINK, DESIRE, DESPAIR...

THERE'S DOUBT THAT OCCURS ONLY IN BIG HOSPITALS AT NIGHT, UNEASE FELT AT NO OTHER PLACE OR TIME.

LOST IN ANTISEPTIC HALLS, TURNING CORNERS, COMING FACE TO FACE WITH THINGS WE SHOULD NOT HAVE SAID; DONE; THOUGHT; ALLOWED TO HAPPEN.

SOMEWHERE ELSE A WOMAN LOWS. A BLANCHED MALE VOICE ASKS "HOW MUCH DID HE TAKE," BUT NO ONE ANSWERS, NO ONE ANSWERS.

FOUR-LANE SMASH ARRIVING IN THE LOBBY, DAZED MAN HUGGING BARBIE DOLL...THIS IS A HOUSE OF WOUNDS, AND OF UNLIKELY STORIES.

SOME PEOPLE OCCUR ONLY IN BIG HOSPITALS AT NIGHT, TRYING TO RATIONALIZE LIFE'S WRECKAGE...

STRUGGLING TO ACCEPT DEATH'S NEW PROXIMITY.

9

I'M SORRY, MR. WILLIAMS, BUT OUR COMPUTER LISTS NO *"MATT CAMBELL"!*

THAT'S *CABLE.* C-A-B-L...

...STRAIGHT DOWN THE CORRIDOR AND ACROSS THE INTERSECTION. MRS. MONROE IS AT THE END.

UH, EXCUSE ME A MOMENT, I'LL BE RIGHT *BACK.*

INFORMA[TION]

WALLACE? WALLACE MONROE?

HEY MAN, *SYNCHRONICITY!* YOU REMEMBER *ME?*

CHESTER *WILLIAMS.* WE MET UP IN *GOTHAM* LAST FALL.

WHY *YES.*

YES, *I* REMEMBER. YOU GAVE ME THAT SLICE OF *SWEET POTATO* TO GIVE TO MY WIFE. HOW *STRANGE* RUNNING INTO YOU *NOW.*

WELL, I'M JUST HERE *LOOKING* FOR SOMEBODY.

UHH...HOW *IS YOUR* WIFE?

DYING. BUT I GOT UP THE COURAGE TO COME SEE HER A COUPLE OF TIMES. GAVE HER YOUR PIECE OF *YAM,* TOLD HER TO TRY IT IF THINGS GOT *BAD.*

WOW.

DID SHE *TAKE* IT?

91 ○ 104

WELL, THE HOSPITAL CALLED TODAY AND SAID SHE'D LOST CONSCIOUSNESS, BUT SEEMED *ECSTATIC,* MUMBLING ABOUT *LIGHT AND ANGELS* AND JESUS.

I *HOPE* SHE TOOK IT, HOPE I EASED HER SUFFERING.

UROLOGY→

BUT THEN, I REMEMBER THE POISON *KILLING* HER, THE POISON I HELPED *SPREAD,* AND I KNOW IT'S NOT *ENOUGH.*

HAZARD!

DEPT. OF RADIOLOGY

10

THEY SAID I SHOULD COME *QUICKLY*, THAT SHE MAY NOT HAVE *LONG*...

I'D NEED *DECADES* TO MEND THE DAMAGE I'VE DONE.

UHH, WELL, MAYBE YOU DON'T WANNA THINK ABOUT THIS RIGHT *NOW*, BUT I'M IN THIS GROUP TRYING TO MEND *ENVIRONMENTAL* DAMAGE.

HERE'S OUR NUMBER.

UH...WELL, THANK YOU. PERHAPS I'LL CALL.

I MEAN, I'M EXPECTING A LOT OF TIME TO MYSELF QUITE *SOON*.

UH... SURE. WELL, LOOK, YOU TAKE *CARE* NOW. NICE SEEING YOU AGAIN, MAN.

HOPE EVERYTHING'S OKAY WITH THE *WIFE*.

TREASURE?

I'M *SORRY*, MR. *MONROE*, WE TRIED TO CALL YOU, BUT YOU'D ALREADY LEFT THE HOUSE.

SHE WOKE BRIEFLY. SHE SAID TO TELL YOU SHE WAS SORRY SHE COULDN'T *WAIT*, AND TO THANK YOU FOR *SHOWING* HER SO MUCH.

SHE SAID TO TELL YOU "*GOODNIGHT*."

11

RED SOX

PAULIE SKINNER COULD SLEEP FOREVER. THIS LEAVE HAD BEEN THAT LONG IN COMING. IT'D BEEN DUE AFTER GOTHAM, BUT *NOOOOO*: THEY NEEDED A NAPALM SPECIALIST IN HONDURAS TRAINING CONTRAS, AND HE WAS IT.

FINALLY THEN, HOME TO CONNECTICUT; MOM; HIS OLD ROOM; THAT OLD PEACH TREE OUTSIDE...

AS HIS MOTHER TUCKS HIM IN, THE KILLER SIGHS.

SLIPPERING SOFTLY FROM THE ROOM, SHE SAYS SHE'LL BRING HIM COCOA LATER, IF HE'S STILL AWAKE, AND THE KILLER SAYS "THANKS, MA."

HE CUPS ONE HAND BETWEEN HIS LEGS, THE WAY HE'S PREFERRED TO SLEEP SINCE CHILDHOOD.

THE PEACH BLOSSOM SMELLS BEAUTIFUL TONIGHT.

SWEET AND DEEP WITH MEMORIES, ITS PERFUME WHORES ALONG THE EVENING BREEZE.

THE SMALL, PALE FLAKES DRIFT IN HIS OPEN WINDOW, AND, UPON THE PRECIPICE OF SLEEP, THE KILLER THINKS HOW MUCH IT LOOKS LIKE SOMETHING OUT OF "BAMBI"; SMILES; SHUTS HIS EYES.

THE SCENTED MOONLIGHT IN HIS ROOM CREEPS OVER HIM DELICIOUSLY, SO THICK YOU COULD WRING SYRUP FROM IT, AND HE SLEEPS.

IN THE DREAM, PAULIE SKINNER IS FIVE YEARS OLD, SITTING WITH HIS MOTHER IN SHADE BENEATH THE PEACH TREE.

HER DRESS IS CANDY-RIBBON SILK, PINK AND SHINY.

HER KNEE IS SLIPPERY.

SHE'S WEARING SOME SORT OF PERFUME THAT SMELLS CHEAP AND SICKLY. HE DOESN'T LIKE IT.

IT GETS STRONGER ANYWAY.

12

HE TRIES TO WRIGGLE AWAY BUT SHE PULLS HIM CLOSER, HIS HANDS SINK INTO THE PINK SILK PLUMPNESS OF HER BODY, BONELESS AS A CUSHION...

THE PERFUME IS EVERYWHERE NOW.

HELL-O-OOO? PAULIE, 'R YOU STILL *AWAKE?*

I BROUGHT YOU SOME COCOA, LIKE I PRO...

13

OUTSIDE AN AMBULANCE BEGINS TO SCREAM AS IF OVERWHELMED BY THE SUFFERING IT MUST FOREVER CARRY IN ITS BELLY.

SHE TRIES TO CATCH A GLIMPSE OF THE MAN SHE ONCE THOUGHT SHE'D DIE SOONER THAN LOSE, BUT HE'S NOT THERE.

IT'S AS IF HE'S SLIPPED BENEATH THE SURFACE OF HIS OWN LIFE.

THAT SURFACE IS FROZEN NOW, TWO YEARS THICK. JUST LIKE A FISH BENEATH THE ICE HE'S HARD TO SEE, IMPOSSIBLE TO REACH.

STANDING, SHE PULLS HER BELT TIGHT ENOUGH TO HURT, FOR NO GOOD REASON.

THE ICE BETWEEN THEM'S DIAMOND HARD, IMPERVIOUS. IT WILL NOT CRACK, HOWEVER FIERCE OR DESPERATE THE BLOW, BUT SOMETIMES MELTS A LITTLE...

JUST ENOUGH TO WET THEM BOTH.

14

HEY! ABBY! I FINALLY *CONNECTED* WITH YOU!

LIZ TOLD ME YOU WERE HERE. I FIGURED I'D COME *OVER.*

ALL VISIT MUS REGI A DES

HOW'S THINGS WITH YOUR, UH, YOUR *EX-HUSBAND?*

OH, WELL, HE TOLD ME ABOUT THE *MOVIES* HE'D SEEN, AND WE DISCUSSED *POLITICS* AND HE SAID HE LIKED MY *OUTFIT...*

REALLY?

NO.

LOOK, I'M *SORRY.* SINCE *ALEC* DIED, COMING HERE TO SEE *MATT,* I JUST FEEL *EMPTY,* LIKE I DON'T HAVE ENOUGH STUFF TO MOURN BOTH OF THEM.

DO YOU MIND IF WE SKIP THE ECO-BUSINESS TONIGHT? I WANT TO DRIVE OUT TO THE SWAMPS.

YOU WANT TO BE *ALONE?*

ALONE?

CHESTER, LATELY I'VE BEEN WORKING WITH *OLD* PEOPLE, WHOSE KIDS HAVE STUCK THEM IN A HOME WITH A LOT OF PEOPLE THEY DON'T *KNOW* AND I JUST THINK *"CHRIST,"* YOU KNOW?

NO...

NO, I DON'T WANT TO BE ALONE.

TERREBONNE GENERAL HOSPITAL AMBULANCE

AM

TERRE

⑮

"MR. CUTLEY IS WORKING ALONE AT THE RETREAT AND DOES NOT WISH TO BE DISTURBED. PLEASE LEAVE YOUR NAME AFTER THE TONE."

THE RINGING IRRITATES HIM. DON'T THEY KNOW ENOUGH TO LEAVE HIM *BE* UP HERE, JUST ONE *WEEKEND?*

PROBABLY SOME UP-AND-CREEPING REPTILE FROM THE *D.D.I.*, LIKE WICKER, OUT TO STEAL HIS JOB, OR EVEN WORSE, CUTLEY'S *NEUROTIC WIFE.*

OUTSIDE, THE WARM MARCH MORNING LOOKS SO *PEACEFUL.*

HE LIKED TO GET UP HERE WHEN THERE WERE SERIOUS PROBLEMS TO BE SOLVED, SEND ALL THE SERVANTS HOME, BE BY HIMSELF.

RIGHT NOW, THE D.D.I. HAD PROBLEMS OUT THE OLD WAZOO.

BUT HOW *BIG* WERE THEY? SURE, THERE'S EVIDENCE TO INDICATE SOME *FILES* WERE BROKEN INTO, BUT NOT MUCH: A SCRAP OF MOSS, MAYBE FROM SOMEONE'S SHOE.

NORMALLY, HE WOULDN'T WORRY, BUT LATELY...

SO MUCH DEPENDED ON HOW FAR THIS WHOLE *IRANGATE* THING WAS GOING TO GO...

...AND HOW MUCH SPILLED OVER ONTO THE D.D.I. THAT WAS ONE OF THE BIG PROBLEMS WITH THIS *BUSINESS.*

NO MATTER WHERE YOU HIDE ALL OF THE CRAP THAT GOES DOWN, HIDE ENOUGH AND THE LEVEL WILL *RISE* 'TIL YOU'RE UP TO YOUR...

16

HIS LAWN IS MAYBE FIFTEEN METERS SQUARE AND CUTLEY KNOWS EVERY FOOT OF IT...

BUT NOT VERTICALLY.

NOT WAITING, NOT DARING TO REFLECT UPON WHAT WAS OCCURRING, HE PUSHES THROUGH THE FLIMSY EMERALD CURTAIN SEEKING REASSURING CONCRETE...

...FINDING THORNS.

CALM. IN CONTROL. THOUGH ALL THE WORLD IS SUDDENLY BERSERK HE MUST STAY IN CONTROL. HE'D TRACE THE WALL ALONG, AND FIND ITS END...

A SUDDEN RIGHT ANGLE MAKES HIM TURN LEFT. HE FINDS AN OPENING IN THE BRIARS, STEPS THROUGH...

...CONTINUES UNTIL HE MEETS A WALL, TURNS RIGHT THEN PANICS AND TRIES TO RETRACE HIS STEPS.

SO: LEFT AND BACK TOWARDS THE BRIAR OPENING, WHICH WAS...

WHERE?

WHERE WAS IT? IT HAD BEEN THERE. IT COULDN'T HAVE CLOSED UP FOR GOD'S SAKE...

THE SERVANTS WOULDN'T BE BACK FOR A WEEK.

HIS LAWN IS MAYBE FIFTEEN METERS SQUARE. A MAN COULDN'T GET LOST ON HIS OWN LAWN!

INSIDE THE HOUSE THE PHONES KEEP RINGING, UNTIL, ONE BY ONE, THEY STOP.

(17)

MR. WICKER? IT'S 1:30. YOU TOLD US TO WAKE YOU WHEN WE BROUGHT IN YOUR LUNCH.

EHUH?

MR. WICKER, IS ALL THIS NECESSARY? WOULDN'T YOU BE MORE COMFORTABLE SLEEPING AT HOME?

LISSEN, SHUDDUPAMINUTE. LEMME...UHH...OKAY.

ONE THIRTY. GOOD. DID THEY REPLACE THE FRONT LAWN WITH ASTROTURF YET? I TOLD THEM NOON...

UH, WELL, LISTEN, ABOUT ALL THAT STUFF, Y'KNOW, THE LOBBY PLANTS, AND THE LAWN...

...IT SEEMS TO US, SIR, THAT... WELL, YOU'VE BEEN UNDER STRESS SINCE THE GOTHAM BUSINESS, AND NOW THIS TROUBLE WITH POOR OLLIE NORTH...

WHAT ARE YOU SAYING? GIVE ME THOSE SANDWICHES.

YOU'RE SAYING I'M NOT FIT TO DO MY JOB?

NOBODY'S SAYING THAT, SIR. BUT... WELL, KILLING ALL THE PLANTS AROUND H.Q....

DAMN STRAIGHT: METAL AND MICA AND PLASTIC FROM NOW ON, AND THAT'S IT, OKAY?

I MEAN, DON'T YOU SEE THE PATTERN? THE COMPUTER WAS BROKEN INTO, ALL THE DETAILS ABOUT GOTHAM...

AND THEN FOLEY! HAVE THE POLICE ALLOWED US ACCESS TO THE GIRL YET?

NO. THEY FOUND HER AND HER PIMP TRYING TO DITCH FOLEY'S BODY, BUT THEY CAN'T GET A STRAIGHT STORY FROM 'EM.

HA! I'LL BET THEY CAN'T!

: GNOF : AND WHAT ABOUT SKINNER? DROWNED IN BLOSSOM! FREAK ACCIDENT MY ASS! HAS ANYONE CONTACTED CUTLEY YET?

SIR, MR. CUTLEY'S AT THE RETREAT...

19

HE'S SORTING THROUGH THE RUBBLE IN THE AFTERMATH OF THE *TOWER* REPORT, AND LEFT INSTRUCTIONS NOT TO BE *DISTURBED*.

HE *HAS* BEEN THERE FOUR *DAYS* NOW...

WELL, THAT'S NOT *UNUSUAL*, GIVEN THE *SCALE* OF THE CRISIS. I'VE KNOWN TIMES IN THE *PAST* HE HASN'T ANSWERED THE PHONE ALL *WEEK* UP THERE.

HIS *WIFE* CALLED.

SHE *DID*? WHAT WAS IT *THIS* TIME? A *PROWLER*? A *UFO*? CHRIST, THEY OUGHTA GIVE HER STRONGER *TABLETS*.

SHE HAD A *DREAM*, ABOUT *CUTLEY*. WANTS US TO *REACH* HIM...

AAA, SHE'S AFRAID HE'S GOT SOME *SECRETARY* UP THERE AT THE *RETREAT* WITH HIM!

WELL, SHE SOUNDED *WORRIED* ABOUT HIM...

SHE SAID "*PHONE* HIM. TELL HIM NOT TO GET LOST. I *DREAMED* HE GOT LOST."

A WIFE LIKE *THAT*, I'D WANNA GET LOST.

YOU DIDN'T *HEAR* HER. SHE...

WAIT A MINUTE, MAN.

MR. *WICKER*? YOU *OKAY*?

EVERYTHING ALL RIGHT WITH YOUR *LUNCH*?

RON, LOOK *OUT*, HE'S...

HEY! HEY, MR. *WICKER*? WHAT'S THE *MATTER*? SIR, TELL US WHAT...

GNNH

EKKEHH

DON, FOR CHRIST'S SAKE *SHOOT* IT!

SHOOT *WHAT*? WHAT AM I GONNA *SHOOT*? OH CHRIST, OH JESUS, LOOK AT HIS *SHIRT*! WHAT'S...

AGHHEH

HELP. WE GOTTA GET *HELP*...

EAGLE'S NEST? EAGLE'S NEST THIS IS LION'S GODDAMN *DEN*. WE GOT ...OH JEEZ, JUST GET SOMEBODY *DOWN* HERE!

OH GOD. OH *NO*...

HHEEHHHGHH

HHHGGHHUHH

OH SH...

HELLO, LION'S DEN? LION'S DEN, THIS IS EAGLE'S NEST. DO YOU *COPY*?

20

A-ABBY?

ABBY, I...I *FOUND* SOMETHING...

YEAH, WELL, I'M NOT *INTERESTED.* I ALREADY GOT A LIFE THAT MOST PEOPLE WOULD NEED DRUGS TO *IMAGINE.* I MEAN, WITH ACQUAINTANCES LIKE *MINE,* WHO NEEDS *HALLUCINATIONS?*

BUT...LOOK, I FOUND ALL *THESE.* IN THIS LIGHT, IT'S DIFFICULT TO BE *SURE,* BUT I THINK THEY LOOK LIKE...

SEE, THE *COLOR* IS THE SAME, AND THAT APRICOT, FUZZY SORT OF FEEL TO THE SKIN, BUT...

BUT, WELL, THESE *CAN'T* BE THE SAME TUBERS. EVEN IF HE DROPPED 'EM HERE ALL THAT *TIME* AGO...

I MEAN, THEY'D HAVE *ROTTED* BY NOW. BUT THEN THE *SMELL'S* SO SIMILAR...THAT STUFF THEY USE IN INDIAN *COOKERY,* TASTES KINDA *SCENTED.* WHAT'S IT CALLED? I CAN'T...

UH, ABBY? WHAT'S...

OH.

OH *WOW.*

ABBY, I...I THINK I'M HAVING SOME KIND OF *FLASH-BACK.*

OH JEEZ. THIS...

THIS IS REAL.

WHAT...WHAT *IS* IT? IS IT AN *EARTHQUAKE?* COME ON, WE GOTTA GET *OUT.* WE GOTTA...

ABBY! LOOK OUT, THE EARTH IS...

...IS...

ABBY?

23

NEXT:
RETURN OF THE GOOD GUMBO

PLIK.

THE MORNING'S
EDGE BLURS INTO
RIVER FOG. A
SMOLDERING FRIEZE,
THE DISTANT
BANKS CRAWL BY.

BLOP.

THE CLOUDY PANES
OF WATER SHATTER
QUIETLY, AND SINGLE
BIRD-NOTES SWIM AWAY
ACROSS THE SURFACE,
MERGING WITH THE EERIE
SOUNDTRACK OF THE
WATERWAYS.

SHLIP.

SPITTING A JEWEL OF
GREEN INTO GREEN
DEPTHS, GENE LABOSTRIE
SHOULDERS HIS CRAFT
INTO A CLOCKLESS,
DROWNED CONTINUUM.
IMPALED UPON HIS POLE,
THE WATER WRITHES.

BLOP.
BETWEEN THE TREES HE WAS PERHAPS
CONCEIVED BENEATH HE PAUSES,
SQUINTING UP. CUT BY A JET PLANE'S
WING THE SKY MOANS FOR A WHILE
AND THEN GOES BACK TO SLEEP.

LABOSTRIE
SIGHS; ADJUSTS
HIS HAT; HEADS
ON.

GUP.   PLINC.   BLOP.

1

OUTSIDE THE VILLAGE, YOUNG MEN PRACTICE THE PURSUIT OF A RED ROOSTER, READY FOR THE COMING FAIR.

BREATHLESS, IT FINDS A TREETOP WHILE BELOW THE MOB CONVERGE UPON ITS PERCH.

RESIGNED, TOO TIRED TO FLY AWAY, THE BIRD SITS WATCHING AS THE SHOUTING BOYS RISE UP THE TREE LIKE BRUSHFIRE.

TOSSED HIGH ABOVE THE STRUGGLING CROWD, THE DOOMED BIRD FLUTTERS, BOUNCING OFF ACROSS THE DEW-CHILLED GRASS.

LaBOSTRIE WONDERS, CAN THIS WAY OF LIFE ENDURE FOREVER, OR MUST THE PERSISTENT DRIP OF MODERN TIMES SOON EAT AWAY THE ROCK OF THEIR TRADITIONS?

OBSCURELY MELANCHOLY, GENE LaBOSTRIE LEAVES THE SLOW ECCENTRIC TIDE TO LULL AND PACIFY HIS TETHERED SKIP.

SLEP.

SLEP.

SLEP.

HE SMELLS HIS WIFE'S STEW, SIMMERING, SOMEHOW LESS TEMPTING BY THE WEEK. THE FISH AND MEAT ARE GOOD, BUT DECENT VEGETABLES SEEM SCARCE.

THERE IS A SAVOR THAT HAS GONE FROM LIFE, SOME NUANCE NOTICED ONLY IN ITS ABSENCE.

OUTSIDE, A WHITE DOG BARKS BARKS BARKS INTO AN EMPTY STREET. THROUGH A GRAY PALL OF COOKING STEAM A LOVELY WOMAN SCOWLS AND TURNS AWAY.

HER CHEAP FIVE-DOLLAR PERFUME WANDERS OUT ALONE INTO THE BAYOU, LIKE A HOPELESS PRAYER.

2

IT IS AS IF THE SPIRIT HAS DEPARTED FROM THIS LAND.

THE CHILDREN CRY AND GIVE NO EXPLANATION. PREMATURELY AGED BY SPANISH MOSS THE TREES STAND SULKING, WAITING FOR A WORD OF RECONCILIATION NO ONE CAN PRONOUNCE.

EACH DAY'S SUN SEEMS LESS WILLING TO BEGIN ITS LABORED, STRUGGLING ASCENT TOWARDS THE SHADELESS PINNACLES OF NOON, LESS EAGER TO DRIVE BACK THE EBB-TIDE NIGHT ACROSS THE SWAMPS AND TURN THEIR MIRROR-RIBBONED STREAMS TO CHROME.

WHERE HAD THEY GONE, THOSE FINE ACCORDION AFTERNOONS; THOSE CRAW-FISH-BAITING NIGHTS?

WERE THEY SNATCHED UP, BORN STRUGGLING ALOFT BETWEEN A HERON'S TOES, OR DID THEY MELT AWAY FOREVER, GONE WHERE SMOKE GOES?

IF LaBOSTRIE COULD RISE ABOVE THE PLANET AND LOOK DOWN, WOULD HE SEE THIS AFFLICTION REACHING EVERY-WHERE?

MAD JOY AND SWEETNESS FELT SO UNAPPRECIATED BY THIS WORLD THAT THEY'D WITH-DRAWN ENTIRELY FROM OUR LIVES?

HOW CAN WE MAKE AMENDS? WHAT MUST WE DO BEFORE FATE, GLANCING DOWN, TAKES PITY AND DECIDES TO THROW US BACK THE THINGS WE'VE LOST?

OUR LOVE. OUR HEARTS. THE MEANING IN OUR LIVES. LIFE'S PASSIONS...

ALL ITS UNEXPECTED BEAUTIES.

3

RETURN OF THE GOOD GUMBO

SWAMP THING

CREATED BY
LEN WEIN & BERNI WRIGHTSON

ALAN MOORE
writer
STEVE BISSETTE
TOM YEATES
RICK VEITCH &
ALFREDO ALCALA
Artists
KAREN BERGER
Editor
TATJANA WOOD: colorist
JOHN COSTANZA: letterer

④

MMMM.

I NEVER *FELT* THIS HAPPY, NOT IN MY WHOLE *LIFE!* I...I'M ALMOST GLAD I *LOST YOU,* JUST TO GET YOU *BACK.*

THEN... OUR *SEPARATION...*HAS LEFT...NO LASTING *SCARS...?*

NO. I FEEL *STRONGER,* KNOWING I *CAN* SURVIVE WITHOUT YOU...

...JUST LIKE I FEEL *DELIRIOUS* KNOWING I DON'T *HAVE* TO.

YES. THE MONTHS *APART...* HAVE ALSO BEEN... A TIME OF GROWTH... FOR *ME.* I'VE BEEN SO *FAR...*AND LEARNED SO *MUCH...*

"THE BLUE WORLD...WHERE I LEARNED... JUST HOW *INSIDIOUS* A TRAP...IS *SOLITUDE...*"

"THAT MAD HALF-LIVING / HALF-MACHINE ENVIRONMENT... THAT MAY HAVE BEEN A *NIGHTMARE...*SUFFERED BETWEEN WORLDS..."

"THE *FASCINATING* FLORA-CULTURE OF JS86..."

"THE *STERILE WASTES* OF *RANN...* WHERE I HELPED THEM TO END *THEIR...*"

...BUT THAT IS *ENOUGH.* I SHALL NOT *BORE* YOU... WITH MY TALES OF *SPACE...*

...WHILE *THIS* WORLD PROMISES... SO VERY *MUCH...*

YEAH. ISN'T IT A LOVELY *DAY?* THIS IS THE FIRST WEEK OF *SPRING,* YOU KNOW?

UH, I GUESS YOU *DID,* RIGHT?

5

I GUESS *EARTH ELEMENTALS* PROBABLY GET NOTIFIED *FIRST* ABOUT THINGS LIKE THAT.

GEE. LOOK AT THE RIVER, WITH ALL THAT *MIST.* TOO BAD WE DON'T HAVE A *BOAT.*

OH...I THINK...WE COULD *ARRANGE* ONE...

WHERE *FROM?* WE CAN'T JUST...

ALEC? WHAT ARE YOU DOING?

SOME *MINOR...* *STRUCTURAL* WORK...

DON'T...BE *ALARMED...*

GLAK

PLUTCH

FLET

BUT WHAT...OOOHHH! HAHAHAHAHA!

ALEC, THAT'S *GREAT!* WILL IT *WORK?*

FELCH

GLOT

SLUK

PLEC

WHY NOT *TRY* IT... AND SEE...?

WHUUUP

HEY! HOLD IT *STEADY* THERE. I DON'T HAVE ANYTHING TO HOLD *ON* TO...

OKAY.

OKAY, I'M IN. TAKE IT AWAY.

6

THE HEAT OF HER BREASTS...OF HER LOINS...SINKS THROUGH THE LICHENS... OF MY FLATTENED SHOULDERS... MORE WARMING...THAN THE HALF-AWAKENED SUN. WE DRIFT...IN AN INTIMATE...ELOQUENT SILENCE...

...A SILENCE... I AM ODDLY GRATEFUL FOR...

WHY DID I HESITATE...?

WHY DIDN'T I REVEAL... WHAT I'D DONE UPON RANN, PREVENTING FAMINE...

SHOULD I NOT FEEL PROUD?

ABBY TUGS SHARPLY... ON MY MOSS, AND POINTS...

GATORS. I HEAD... TOWARDS THE BANK...

HAD I AVOIDED MENTIONING... MY CAPABILITIES BECAUSE...?

BECAUSE THERE'S FAMINE HERE ON EARTH? BECAUSE...I MIGHT BE ASKED...TO END THAT TOO? BUT THEN...WHY NOT?

I SET HER DOWN... STILL NEEDING TIME... TO THINK...

PERHAPS A MOMENT'S SPORT...PROVIDING ME WITH A REPRIEVE... AN INTERLUDE... IN WHICH TO PUT MY THOUGHTS IN ORDER... LEARN WHY THIS OMISSION...SHOULD SO TROUBLE ME...

PULLING ON LIMBS... AS IF THEY WERE A BATHING COSTUME...I WADE OUT...

...AND INTO DEPTHS AS MURKY...AND DISTURBED...AS THOSE WITHIN MY HEART...

I COULD END FAMINE...HERE... ON EARTH. THOSE CHILDREN... STARVING... DYING AT THIS MOMENT...

WHY... DON'T I... JUST TELL HER?

CORRODED TIN CANS FREE-FALL ROUND MY FEET... AS I WALK ON... INTO THE SHIFTING GLOOM...

7

ONE OF THE MONSTERS HUNTS FOR ME...DROPPING BENEATH THE WATER... WITH A STRANGLER'S SILENCE...BELLYING THROUGH THE UMBER, RIVER-BOTTOM CLOUDS AN IRON-GREEN TORPEDO...HIDDEN FROM ALL SIGHT, YET DANGEROUS...LIKE A SUPPRESSED ANXIETY...

ENCIRCLING ITS COLD, SLICK GIRTH...WITH ARMS DESIGNED TO HOLD...ABUNDANT FRUITS ALOFT FOR CENTURIES...I WRESTLE WITH IT...STRUGGLING TO DEFINE BY TOUCH ...A SHAPE OBSCURED BY SEPIA...

I COULD DO IT.

I COULD RESTORE AFRICA'S CRUMBLING TOPSOIL....TO THE LOAM FROM WHICH...RICH JUNGLES SPRANG...

...AND WHY STOP THERE? WHY NOT REBUILD THE FORESTS...OF THE AMAZON...LESS GREEN NOW...THAN AN AVERAGE SUBURBIA...AND SHRINKING BY THE DAY.

THE CONCEPT...WRITHES UNCOMFORTABLY...WITHIN MY GRASP...BUT I HOLD TIGHT...

I COULD DROP GRAPES...INTO THE MOUTHS...OF ALL THE HUNGRY CHILDREN...TURN THE GOBI AND SAHARA...INTO GREEN AND RIPPLING MEADOWS...GIVE THE WIDOWS ROSES...AND THE OLD MEN STRAWBERRIES...

FOR AM I NOT A GOD? I COULD TOUCH ALL THE WORLD...WITH GORGEOUS WILDERNESS...AS I TOUCHED GOTHAM...COULD TRANSFORM THIS PLANET...TO A SPHERE OF COLORS...PERFUMES...AND FULL BELLIES.

I COULD SAVE MANKIND.

I COULD DO ANYTHING.

8

MIND STILL REELING... BRIEFLY SATED WITH EXHILARATION... I LET THE ENTIRE SUBJECT DROP... WATCHING IT FALL AWAY BENEATH ME... GOING BACK TO THRUST ITS SNOUT...INTO THE SILT AND SEDIMENT...OF THE MIND'S LOWER REACHES, WHENCE IT CAME...

MY VICTORY ASSURED...I LET IT GO...

...FOR THE MOMENT.

HEY! THAT WAS GREAT! YOU LOOKED LIKE ROY ROGERS...

...WELL, YOU KNOW, IF YOU LEFT HIM IN A DARK CORNER OF THE REFRIGERATOR FOR A COUPLE MONTHS.

AND I LIKED TRIGGER, TOO. CAN WE ADOPT ONE LIKE THAT?

NOT UNLESS...YOU WISH TO BE THE ONE... WHO TRIES TO FLUSH IT... DOWN THE TOILET... WHEN YOU'RE BORED WITH IT...

SHALL WE...WALK SOME MORE...?

SURE. ROY AND DALE HITTING THE HAPPY TRAILS TOGETHER, RIGHT. Ha-pee Traaaails TT to YOOO...

UMMF: Y'KNOW, THIS ECOLOGY WORK, YOU'D REALLY BE PROUD OF US...

I CANNOT IMAGINE... ANY CIRCUMSTANCES... WHERE I WOULD NOT... BE PROUD OF YOU...

CHESTER WAS PLAYING THAT THE LAST TIME WE HAD AN ECO GROUP MEETING AT HIS PLACE IN BATON ROUGE...

HERE I COME. DON'T DROP ME...

AAAH, YOU SAY THAT BECAUSE YOU'RE TOO CHEAP TO BUY CHOCOLATES.

NO, SERIOUSLY, THERE WAS TALK ABOUT DUMPING WASTE HERE, BUT WE KICKED UP SO THEY ABANDONED THE IDEA.

UH, WELL, THAT IS, THEY DUMPED IT SOMEPLACE ELSE.

10

SEE, THAT'S *IT:* YOU HOLD THE LINE *ONE* PLACE, YOUR PROBLEM'S JUST DUMPED ON SOME *OTHER* PERSON'S DOORSTEP.

SOMETIMES I THINK FOR US TO *REALLY* HELP THE ENVIRONMENT, WE'D NEED A DIFFERENT *WORLD*...

SOMEPLACE THAT TAUGHT PEOPLE HOW EVERYTHING FROM THE ENVIRONMENT TO POLITICS WAS *CONNECTED,* TAUGHT THEM TO *THINK* AND TAKE *RESPONSIBILITY*...

I SEE PEOPLE *WORKING* ON THAT, BUT IT NEVER GETS OFF THE *GROUND.*

YOU SHOULD NOT BE... *DISPIRITED*...

PERHAPS THIS NEW *WORLD*... IS CLOSER THAN YOU *THINK*... READY TO SOAR ALOFT... FROM THE ASHES OF THE *OLD.*

YEAH. I GUESS YOU'RE *RIGHT.* IT'S *OUR* PLANET. WE CAN *SAVE* IT, IF WE *TRY* HARD ENOUGH.

SHE SHOOTS A QUESTION- ING GLANCE... BUT DOES NOT PRESS THE MATTER... KNOWING I'LL SPEAK FURTHER WHEN I'M READY... KNOWING ME... KNOWING ALL OF MY WAYS...

THAT WAS NOT QUITE... WHAT I MEANT.

WE WALK... THE TREES LENDING OUR SILENCE FORM... AN EASTER ISLAND HUSH, OBSERVED IN DEFERENCE... TO THESE GIANT, ANCIENT PRESENCES.

SINCE MY RETURN WE'VE KISSED... SPOKEN... EMBRACED... AND NOTHING MORE.

THE THING UNDONE... HANGS IN THE AIR BETWEEN US... INVESTING THAT MOST SLENDER SPACE... WITH MORE SIGNIFI- CANCE... THAN WE OURSELVES POSSESS.

ONLY WHEN OUR DISPLACED DESIRE... SEEMS TO CHARGE EVERY BREEZE... AND BLADE OF GRASS... DO WE STOP WALKING...

FACE EACH OTHER...

SMILE.

11

SHE LOVES ME...

MAKING TINY MEASURED CRIES...AS IF SLOWLY IMMERSED...IN WATER THAT'S TOO ICY. OR TOO HOT...HER FINGERS SCRABBLE...UNLEASHED DOGS UPON MY PARK-GREEN BACK. SHREDDED AND CRUSHED...SMALL LEAVES AND PETALS FALL...

SHE LOVES ME NOT.

I AM THE LIMPET-ARMORED ROCK...SHE IS THE TIDE...THE WHITE FOAM STREAMING DOWN HER NECK...HER SHOULDERS...SEA AND SHORE WE CLASH TOGETHER...FALL ASUNDER...CLASH TOGETHER, FALL...

SHE LOVES ME.

THERE IS A TENDER JUNCTION...WHERE THE WORLDS OF PLANT AND ANIMAL CONVERSE...I AM THE VELDT... HER MUSCLES FLOW ACROSS ME LIKE A HERD...OF SLEEK AND LEAPING IBEX...AND SHE'S HOWLING LIKE A ZOO...SHE'S SCREAMING LIKE A JUNGLE FIRE...

SHE LOVES ME NOT.

HER WORLD AND MINE... LOCKED INTO A COLLISION ORBIT.. SPINNING FASTER...WINDING TIGHTER...DESPERATE FOR OUR FINAL IMPACT...OUR SUBLIME APOCALYPSE, AND OH

AND OH

AND OH

AND OH

AND OH SHE LOVES ME.

13

...AND HAVING... LOVED... SHE SLEEPS.

IT IS A HUMAN THING... TO AFFIRM LIFE SO FIERCELY AND SO PHYSICALLY... SURRENDERING THE BODY... TO SOME ANCIENT AND VESTIGIAL PELVIC BRAIN... AND, HAVING DONE THIS... TO ALLOW ALL SUCH VITALITY TO CEASE... TO STRIKE A CONTRAST... BETWEEN THOSE RED, CARNAL MOMENTS... AND THE BLUE, ENDURING COMA-HOURS...

IT IS A HUMAN THING.

...BUT I AM NOT... AND WHILE SHE SLEEPS... I LIE AWAKE...

THOUGH FLESH MUST REST... SUCH ANIMAL REQUIREMENTS ARE BEHIND ME NOW... MY ONLY HUMAN URGES THOSE... THAT I MYSELF HAVE CHOSEN TO RETAIN...

THE REST WERE BURNED WITH ALEC HOLLAND... ON THE NIGHT HE DIED... THE NIGHT HIS COZY, REASSURING WORLD ERUPTED... BLOSSOMED INTO AN ENORMOUS ROSE OF PURGING FIRE...

...AND HE WENT DOWN INTO THE SWAMP... FALLING AWAY BENEATH ITS SURFACE... BURNING STILL... A HALF-SPENT NAVAL FLARE THAT BLAZED LIKE LIFE ITSELF... SPUTTERED... AND FINALLY WENT OUT...

THE SWAMP DEVOURED HIM... THROUGH A THOUSAND MOUTHS OF RUSSET GREEN... REDUCED HIM TO A CARCASS... ALGAE-SPATTERED... PITIFUL... PICKED CLEAN... YET FROM THOSE WRETCHED LEFTOVERS... THERE CAME A WOODLAND GOD... SUCH AS THERE HAD AT OTHER TIMES... ON COUNTLESS PREVIOUS OCCASIONS... WITH EVENTS SIMILARLY CONTRIVED...

...ENDING WITH ROASTED MEN... AT REST UPON A RIVER BED...

14

WHEN WITH THE PARLIAMENT OF TREES... DOWN BY THE SLOW GREEN TEFE'S SOURCE... I GLIMPSED WITHIN THEIR MINDS A DYNASTY... SPANNING THE EONS... REACHING BACK TO TIMES BEFORE MANKIND... WHOSE ONLY RECORD NOW... IS ETCHED ON SHEETS OF COAL, FAR UNDERGROUND...

A DYNASTY OF GODS... YET, GODS WHO'VE CHOSEN NEVER TO EXERT THEIR POWER... CONTENT TO SIT AND STARE... INTO THE SHIMMERING BLUE BRAZILIAN SKY... AND GAZE UNBLINKING... AT THE FURIOUS EYE... OF THE MONSOON...

IN THE PRECAMBRIAN... WHEN ALL THE WORLD WAS WEEDS... AND NOTHING CRAWLED... OR SWAM... OR FLEW... THE EARTHGODS RULED THE LAST NON-VIOLENT ERA...'TIL THE SUN GROWS RED AND SWOLLEN ...AND ALL LIFE IS FLED...

THEY COULD HAVE MADE THEIR KINGDOM OF THE PLANTS... AS PERFECT AS I'LL MAKE THIS WORLD OF MEN... AND THERE WOULD NEVER HAVE BEEN NEED... FOR ANY OTHER FORM OF LIFE. THEY COULD HAVE KEPT... THIS PLANET FOR THEIR OWN... AND YET DID NOT...

I WONDER WHY?

INSTEAD... THEY LET THE FISH GLIDE IN... UPON THE WILD, SILURIAN TIDE... AND TOOK THEIR FORMS.... AND PLAYED WITH THEM... YET NEVER MADE THIS WORLD A COOL PISCEAN PARADISE...

...NOR WHEN THE FISH WITH LEGS BOILED UP... FROM THE DEVONIAN MUD... DID THEY IMPOSE REPTILIAN UTOPIA... BUT WATCHED INSTEAD... DELIGHTING IN THE DAZZLING DIVERSITY... OF SHAPES AND SHADES...

15

COMPOSED OF CYCADS AND JURASSIC FERNS...THEY'D IMITATE THE UPSTART BEASTS... FRIGHTENING THUNDER-LIZARDS OFF... WITH THUNDER OF THEIR OWN...

IN THE CRETACEOUS...WHEN THE EARTH GREW TIRED OF SAURIANS...ERASING THEM WITH FROST...TURNING HER HAND INSTEAD TO APES AND CHERRY TREES.... HER GUARDIANS MADE NO MOVE.... TO STAY THAT HAND...AND LET THE AGE OF DINOSAURS ENDURE...

...BUT MOURNED THEIR LOSS...WHILE FINDING CONSOLATION... IN THE EARTH'S FIRST FLOWERS.... SPRUNG FROM THE MUD... WHERE THOSE VAST BODIES FELL.

IS THIS, THEN, WHAT IT IS TO BE A GOD?

TO KNOW, AND NEVER DO? TO WATCH THE WORLD WIND BY... AND IN ITS WINDINGS FIND CONTENT...?

IF I SHOULD FEED THE WORLD... HEAL ALL THE WOUNDS MAN'S SMOLDERING INDUSTRIES HAVE MADE... WHAT WOULD HE DO? WOULD HE RENOUNCE....THE WEALTH HIS SAWMILLS BRING...STEP GENTLY ON THE FLOWERS INSTEAD...AND PLUCK EACH APPLE WITH RESPECT... FOR THIS ABUNDANT WORLD...IN ALL ITS PROVIDENCE...?

NO.

HE WOULD PUMP MORE POISONS... BUILD MORE MINES... SAFE IN THE KNOWLEDGE THAT I STOOD ON HAND... TO MEND THE BIOSPHERE... ENDLESSLY COVERING THE SCARS... HE COULD NOW ENDLESSLY INFLICT.

SOMEWHERE THE PARLIAMENT STAND ROOTED...INERT AND OMNIPOTENT... WHILE TINY SPIDERS DRAPE THEIR RIBS IN SILK...

AFTER THIS NIGHT OF REVERIE...AT LAST I COMPREHEND THEIR STANCE.

16

I CANNOT MEND THE WORLD...WITHOUT COMMITTING GREATER WRONG...YET HAVE NO WISH...TO BE ETERNALLY...EXPOSED TO ALL ITS PAINS...

MANKIND MUST STAND OR FALL...BY ITS MERITS ALONE...SAVE FOR THIS ONE.

THIS ONE I'LL KEEP WITH ME...UNTIL SHE DIES...BEYOND, IF I AM ABLE...

HER EYELIDS FLUTTER...MOTHS THAT STRUGGLE...TO ESCAPE SLEEP'S VIVID MIRE...

I SIT AND THINK ON THIS...THEN...HAVING MADE MY TERRIBLE DECISION...THINK NO MORE.

SHE BREAKFASTS ON FRESH FRUIT...I WATCH HER WIPE JUICE FROM HER CHIN...LEAVING A GLAZE...OF TIGHTENED SKIN...UPON HER HAND'S BACKSIDE...AND AFTER THAT...WE WALK.

SHE SMILES. WE KISS...TASTING THE NEW DAY...SAMPLING ALL ITS FLAVORS...ALL ITS PROMISES...

GEE, THIS IS NICE. HOW LONG'S IT GONNA LAST?

FOREVER...IF YOU WISH...

IF YOU DESIRE...THERE NEED BE NO MORE HORROR...OR ADVENTURE...

WE COULD SIMPLY SETTLE DOWN...LOCATE A PLACE THAT SUITS US BOTH...

OH YEAH? LIKE OVER THERE, MAYBE?

FACE IT, THEY DON'T BUILD DREAM-HOMES OUT IN NEIGHBORHOODS LIKE THIS.

PERHAPS THEY DON'T...

IT MATTERS NOT.

I...DID NOT INTEND...

...TO ASK THEM.

BLUK GLESH   PLUD   SKNEECH

17

"ALEC...? WHAT ARE YOU DOING?"

"WHAT I...SHOULD HAVE DONE... LONG AGO..."

"I'M TIRED...OF QUESTS AND ENEMIES...MANKIND MUST LEARN...TO MANUFACTURE... GLORIES OF ITS OWN...AND TO ATONE...FOR ALL ITS SINS... WITHOUT MY PROMPTING...OR MY AID.

"IT IS...THE ONLY WAY... THEY'LL GROW...

"THE WAY OF THE WOOD.

"BUT...ALL THIS STUFF THAT'S COMING UP. WHAT'S...?"

"IT IS OUR RETIREMENT, ABBY...YOURS AND MINE...BORN OF THE EARTH AS PAYMENT... FOR THE SERVICES WE'VE RENDERED...

"WHY NOT? WHY SHOULD WE TWO... NOT LIVE AS ONE...? IS IT NOT OUR... MOST BASIC RIGHT?

"THE RIGHT OF ALL... HAVE THEY THE WIT... AND GRACE TO SEE IT...BUT THAT IS NOT OUR CONCERN...

"SEE, ABBY...

"SEE HOW ITS COLORS BURN... ALL NEW AND GLISTENING... SEE ITS SMOOTHNESS....AND ITS STRENGTH REVEALED...A SYMPHONY OF LINE...A CHORD OF HARMONY UNITING FORM WITH FUNCTION...AND UTILITY WITH OPULENCE.

"SEE.

"OH.

"OH, ALEC, IT'S...

"CAN WE GO IN? DOES IT HAVE ROOMS? OH, GOD, IT'S JUST LIKE, I DUNNO, A FAIRY TALE OR SOMETHING...

"BUT HOW DO WE REACH IT? DO WE GO AROUND THE BACK, OR...?"

"NO.

"I HAVE ARRANGED...A LILY PAD. HOW ELSE...SHOULD A HANS ANDERSEN PRINCESS... TRANSPORT HERSELF...TO HER CASTLE..."

18

A-ABBY? IS THIS TRUE...?

OH, *LIZ*, I'M SORRY. WHAT WAS I *THINKING* OF? I JUST GOT CAUGHT *UP* IN THE IDEA, AND...

LIZ, FORGIVE ME. I *WON'T* LEAVE YOU ALONE, I *PROMISE.*

UH, WELL, LISTEN, I DUNNO, BUT...

WELL, MAYBE I COULD HELP *OUT.* I, I COULD CALL ON LIZ MOST EVERY *DAY.* I COULD EVEN, *UH...*

WELL, YOU HAVE SOME SPARE *ROOMS* THERE, I COULD EVEN, UH...

WELL, MOVE IN, IF UH, IF LIZ *WANTED* ME TO.

THAT IS.

I... YES.

YES PLEASE.

BUT... I MEAN, ARE YOU SURE?

AND LIKE, WHAT ABOUT THE *ECO GROUP?* THERE'S SO MUCH WORK...

AND THERE'S PLENTY OF PEOPLE TO HANDLE IT. TWO MORE JOINED *TODAY.* YOU REMEMBER THAT *MONROE* GUY I MET AT THE HOSPITAL? HE'S *ONE,* AND SOME WOMAN FROM *NEW ORLEANS.*

DON'T *WORRY,* AB. THE ENVIRONMENT'S SAFE WITH *US.*

YES.

YES...I DO BELIEVE... THAT IT *MIGHT* BE...

A-ALEC?

ALEC *HOLLAND?* I *REMEMBER...*

I REMEMBER I WROTE A *BOOK* ABOUT YOU, IT...IT SOLD LOTS OF *COPIES.*

OH, IT'S SO GOOD TO *SEE* YOU AGAIN...

DO THEY THINK MONEY'S EVERYTHING? THE ONLY YARDSTICK THAT LIFE'S QUALITY IS MEASURED BY?

YES, YES, THEY DO, AND THAT IS WHY THEY ARE SO VERY POOR.

SIGHTING A MOVEMENT ON THE BANKS HE STOPS, THE CURRENT CREASING ON HIS POLE INTO A WIDE AND TRAILING 'V':

THERE...IN THE SHADOWS, SOMETHING MOVES. A MAN...? NO. NO, NOT A MAN.

ARRIVING HOME, GENE LaBOSTRIE WALKS DOWN HIS VILLAGE STREET AND LETS THE LAUGHING CHILDREN TEASE HIM, GRAB-BING AT HIS TRAILING COAT.

IN EVERY GARDEN CABBAGES AND ONIONS GROW SO BIG AND SUCCULENT A MAN MIGHT CRY. THE COOKING SMELLS AND FIDDLE STRAINS ARE TANGLED IN THE SUMMER AIR, BOTH EQUALLY AS SWEET.

GOOD GOD IS IN HIS HEAVEN.

GOOD GUMBO'S IN THE POT.

LaBOSTRIE MOVES HIS BLACK-FRINGED LIPS IN SOMETHING VERY LIKE A PRAYER:

"LAISSEZ LES BONTEMPS ROULER." PLEASE. FOR US. FOR ALL OF US...

LAISSEZ LES BONTEMPS ROULER.

THE END

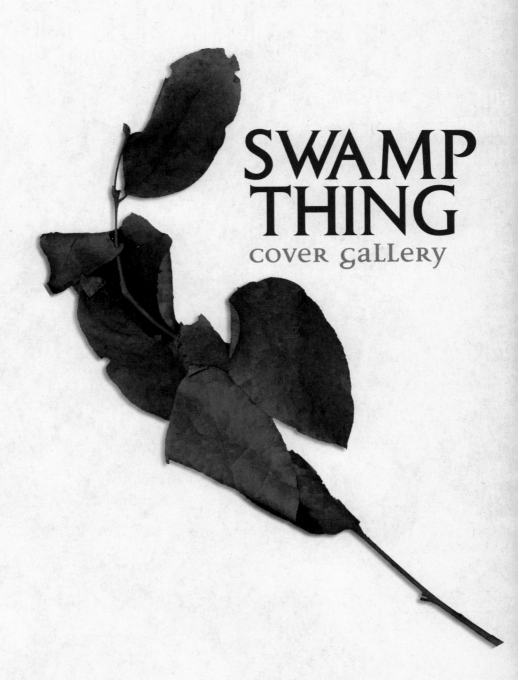

SWAMP THING
cover gallery

75¢
59
APR. 87

SWAMP THING

FOR
MATURE
READERS

TOTLEBEN
1986

COURI

ABIGAIL CABLE
MONSTER LOVER

BY
BISSETTE, MOORE, VEITCH & ALCALA

BRAND NEW FORMAT! SPECIAL PRICE!

SWAMP THING ®

By ALAN MOORE & JOHN TOTLEBEN

61 $1.00
$1.35 CAN
JUN 87
NEW FORMAT

SWAMP THING

MOO
VEITCH
ALCA

SWAMP THING

2
$1.00
$1.35
UK 50p
L 87
NEW FORMAT

CK VEITCH &
LFREDO ALCALA

SWAMP THING

4

$1.00
$1.35 CAN
UK 50p

FORMAT

SUGGESTED
FOR MATURE
READERS

BY
MOORE,
BISSETTE,
YEATES
AND
ALCALA

S.Totleben 2-5-87

BIOGRAPHIES

ALAN MOORE

alan moore began working as a cartoonist in 1979 with several humorous strips in *sounds* music weekly. after a year, he turned to writing, contributing to *doctor who weekly* and *2000ad*. this was followed by *marvelman* (published in the united states as *miracleman*) and the political thriller *v for vendetta*, which earned him the british eagle award for best comics writer in 1982 and 1983. his groundbreaking run on *swamp thing* revolutionized comics and won him several industry awards. he is also the writer of the hugo award-winning *watchmen*, a landmark series that firmly established him as the most influential writer in contemporary comics. in 1999 moore launched his own comics imprint, america's best comics, through which he has created (along with many talented illustrators) *the league of extraordinary gentlemen*, *promethea*, *tom strong*, *tomorrow stories*, and *top ten*.

RICK VEITCH

rick veitch worked in the underground comics scene before attending the joe kubert school of cartoon and graphic art. after graduating, he worked with stephen bissette on *bizarre adventures* before creating and illustrating *the one*, the innovative epic comics miniseries. in addition to writing and drawing an acclaimed run on *swamp thing*, he is the creator/cartoonist of *brat pack*, *maximortal*, and the dream-based *rare bit fiends*, and a contributing artist on *1963*. he is also the writer and artist of the recent miniseries *greyshirt: indigo sunset* from america's best comics, and is the writer behind the newest relaunch of *aquaman* for dc.

STEPHEN BISSETTE

best known for his multi-award-winning tenure on *swamp thing*, stephen bissette also co-founded, edited, and co-published the eisner award-winning controversial horror anthology *taboo*, collaborated with alan moore on *1963*, and wrote, drew, and self-published four issues of *s.r. bissette's tyrant*. bissette's film criticism, articles, and short fiction have appeared in over two dozen periodicals and book anthologies, and his original novella *aliens: tribes* won a bram stoker award in 1993.

JOHN TOTLEBEN

after a childhood in erie, pennsylvania spent consuming a steady diet of comics, monster magazines, and monster movies, john totleben attended the joe kubert school of cartoon and graphic art where he met stephen bissette. together they worked on *bizarre adventures* followed by *swamp thing*, which they drew for almost three years. totleben is best known for his illustrative work on alan moore's *miracleman*. his other credits include *1963*, *vermillion*, and *the dreaming*.

ALFREDO ALCALA

alfredo alcala's graceful, moody inks helped maintain the style on *swamp thing* through many penciller changes. dc first employed alcala's talents in its horror and war comics such as *ghosts*, *unexpected*, and *weird war tales*. he later moved on to titles including *all-star squadron*, *savage sword of conan*, *batman*, *swamp thing* and countless others for both dc and marvel. after a long battle with cancer, alcala passed away in april 2000.

TOM YEATES

born in 1955, tom yeates was one of the first graduates of the joe kubert school of cartoon and graphic art (along with classmates rick veitch, stephen bissette, and john totleben). influenced primarily by the classic adventure illustrators like alex raymond and hal foster, yeates has contributed artwork to a host of titles and publishers, and has served as an editor for eclipse comics as well as illustrating a newspaper strip revival of *zorro* from 1999 to 2000.

TATJANA WOOD

tatjana wood switched careers from dressmaking to comics coloring in the late 1960s and quickly established herself as one of the top colorists in the field, winning two shazam awards in the early 1970s. wood continues to color for dc comics.

JOHN COSTANZA

john costanza entered the comics field in the late 1960s, lettering such groundbreaking series as dennis o'neil and neal adams's *green lantern/green arrow* and jack kirby's *new gods*. in addition to his lettering work, costanza is also an accomplished cartoonist.

THE SWAMP THING LIBRARY

SWAMP THING: DARK GENESIS
LEN WEIN/BERNI WRIGHTSON

SAGA OF THE SWAMP THING
ALAN MOORE/STEPHEN BISSETTE/
JOHN TOTLEBEN

SWAMP THING: LOVE & DEATH
ALAN MOORE/STEPHEN BISSETTE/
JOHN TOTLEBEN/SHAWN MCMANUS

SWAMP THING: THE CURSE
ALAN MOORE/STEPHEN BISSETTE/
JOHN TOTLEBEN

SWAMP THING: A MURDER OF CROWS
ALAN MOORE/VARIOUS

SWAMP THING: EARTH TO EARTH
ALAN MOORE/JOHN TOTLEBEN/
RICK VEITCH/ALFREDO ALCALA

ALSO BY THE SAME AUTHOR

**THE LEAGUE OF
EXTRAORDINARY GENTLEMEN**
Alan Moore/Kevin O'Neill

PROMETHEA: BOOK ONE
Alan Moore/J.H. Williams III/Mick Gray

PROMETHEA: BOOK TWO
Alan Moore/J.H. Williams III/Mick Gray

PROMETHEA: BOOK THREE
Alan Moore/J.H. Williams III/Mick Gray

TOMORROW STORIES: BOOK ONE
Alan Moore/Kevin Nowlan/Rick Veitch/
Jim Baikie/Melinda Gebbie/Hilary Barta

TOM STRONG: BOOK ONE
Alan Moore/Chris Sprouse/Alan Gordon

TOM STRONG: BOOK TWO
Alan Moore/Chris Sprouse/Alan Gordon

TOP TEN: BOOK ONE
Alan Moore/Gene Ha/Zander Cannon

TOP TEN: BOOK TWO
Alan Moore/Gene Ha/Zander Cannon

V FOR VENDETTA
Alan Moore/David Lloyd

WATCHMEN
Alan Moore/Dave Gibbons